DOUBLE
AWESOME
CHINESE
FOOD

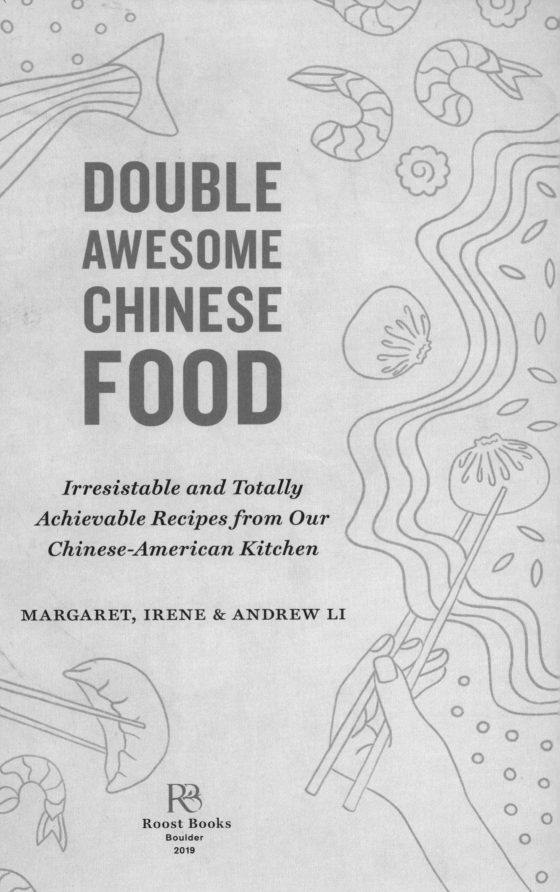

DOUBLE
AWESOME
CHINESE
FOOD

Irresistable and Totally
Achievable Recipes from Our
Chinese-American Kitchen

MARGARET, IRENE & ANDREW LI

Roost Books
Boulder
2019

Roost Books
An imprint of Shambhala Publications, Inc.
4720 Walnut Street
Boulder, Colorado 80301
roostbooks.com

9 8 7 6 5 4 3 2 1

First Edition
Printed in the United States of America

♾ This edition is printed on acid-free paper that meets the
American National Standards Institute Z39.48 Standard.
♻ Shambhala Publications makes every effort to print
on recycled paper. For more information please visit
www.shambhala.com.

Roost Books is distributed worldwide by Penguin Random
House, Inc., and its subsidiaries.

Library of Congress Cataloging-in-Publication Data
Names: Li, Margaret, author. | Li, Irene, author. | Li, Andrew,
author.
Title: Double awesome Chinese food: irresistible and totally
achievable recipes from our Chinese-American kitchen /
Margaret, Irene and Andrew Li.
Description: First edition. | Boulder: Roost Books, 2019. |
Includes index.
Identifiers: LCCN 2017060784 | ISBN 9781611805574
(hardcover: alk. paper)
Subjects: LCSH: Cooking, Chinese. | Cooking—United
States. | Mei Mei (Restaurant) | LCGFT: Cookbooks.
Classification: LCC TX724.5.C5 L51418 2019 | DDC
641.5951—dc23
LC record available at https://lccn.loc.gov/2017060784

Book Design by
Shubhani Sarkar, sarkardesignstudio.com

CONTENTS

INTRODUCTION: A FAMILY STYLE COOKBOOK

family style (adj, adv, n):

a) A method of serving a meal, particularly popular in Chinese cuisine, where dishes are placed in the center of the table and shared by all eaters. Generally includes lots of food passed hand-to-hand, as eaters serve themselves as well as help others.

b) The best way to eat, no matter what kind of food. Everyone gets to try everything. There's no "my food" or "your dish," but an assortment for everyone to enjoy. Eating—along with conversation, laughter, and delight—becomes a communal experience.

c) A cookbook about food, family, and good eating. A story of three siblings—Andrew, Margaret, and Irene. And, of course, the influences of Mom and Dad, grandmas and grandpas, and the rest of our large Chinese-American family.

Let's start with the name Mei Mei. That's really where our idea of family style comes from, where it all begins. *Mei mei* means "little sister" in Mandarin Chinese, the language spoken by our mother's parents and the language our mom and dad valiantly tried to teach us as we grew up just outside Boston. The fun started with Andrew (mostly called Andy), and a scant thirteen months later came his first little sister, Margaret. That's me. Since Margaret was already a mouthful for toddler Andy, I was called Mei Mei at home for years. Growing up, that got shortened to Mei, a nickname that stuck around even when little sister number two, Irene, was born eight years later. Finally, the trio was complete.

Fast-forward twenty-odd years. Andy had been working in hospitality for nearly a decade, moving his way up from nightclub bouncer to front-of-house manager in corporate chains, renowned Boston institutions, and fine-dining restaurants. After years of wearing a suit and observing the complications of the restaurant industry firsthand, he started dreaming of running his own business where he could do things differently (and wear a T-shirt every day). At that point, Irene and I had been exploring the food world for several years, running pop-up restaurants and writing a shared food blog from upstate New York and London, respectively. We called the blog *Family Styles*, to highlight that it was written by sisters and as a nod to the way the family grew up eating, all shared plates and communal dishes. Although both of us were thoroughly enamored with food, we saw our activities as passion projects and not a real career path. But gradually we started discussing more food

business ideas with our big brother, and we realized he was serious about starting a company. The timing made sense for our family—our dad was ill and we all wanted to return to Boston to be with him. Simultaneously, gourmet food trucks were exploding in popularity around the country. Andy asked: *Would we come home to Boston and open a food truck with him?*

We decided on the name Mei Mei to reflect our Chinese heritage and celebrate our sibling relationship. As Irene jokes, we two little sisters agreed to join Andy on his big-wheeled food truck adventure if he'd agree to name the business after us. The food truck has since expanded to include a full-service restaurant and catering company. But in a broader sense, food and family have always been tied together for us. In our family—like many others—every occasion revolved around food, from nightly family dinner to enormous reunions where thirty aunties, uncles, and cousins descend on a Chinese

banquet restaurant for whole fish, duck tongues, and enough white rice to feed an army. Food was the centerpiece of activity; eating was the background to all interactions. In Mandarin Chinese, greeting someone with the question "Have you eaten?" is similar to asking "How are you?" Being well fed is synonymous with a general sense of well-being, an idea that has subtly infused the collective sense of hospitality across our businesses.

Growing up with this feeling of food as love, we've poured our family memories into the dishes we serve at Mei Mei. Our most popular sandwich is based on an enduring childhood love of crispy, golden scallion pancakes—and pesto. The thousands of hand-folded dumplings we sell every week are the contemporary incarnation of the dumplings we folded by hand at our family table. But the fillings—pork, sage and cranberry, mashed potato and sharp cheddar, chorizo and white beans drizzled with cilantro oil—are unconventional combinations that showcase our love for great New England ingredients along with our enthusiasm for crossing boundaries in pursuit of what tastes delicious. Like our Chinese-American upbringing, filled with international influences and multicultural experiences, our food isn't confined to certain notions of authenticity or tradition. Our grandmother might never have dreamed of a Chinese-spiced beef and blue cheese dumpling (cheese was almost unheard of in China in her generation), but we're pretty confident that if she could try one today she'd eat them as enthusiastically as we do.

Our concept of family extends beyond recipes and food memories to encompass so much more than us three siblings. First of all, there's the tour de force that is Mama Mei Mei. Our mom, Elaine, isn't on the payroll, but she's our toughest critic and our best publicist. Our hardworking, fun-loving team, a few of whom have been with us since the week we opened the food truck, represent the next level of the Mei Mei family. And then there's our network of farm partners, fellow food truckers, and restaurant pals

who look out for each other, offer advice, and know a good guy to call when your truck generator fails in the middle of lunch service. They're all family too.

Like any family, we've had our ups and downs. Running a food truck with three opinionated siblings has resulted in both literal and figurative bumps in the road. Despite some heated disagreements, we're thankful for the ways in which we differ as siblings, as these differences ultimately have influenced the strongest tenets of our businesses. Local sourcing, small farms, exclusively pasture-raised meat—that's Irene's contribution from her high school semester on a Vermont farm. Bend-over-backward hospitality for our guests, while also going out of your way for your own staff—that's from Andy's experiences, good and bad, over his decade working in hospitality in Boston. And my entrepreneurial career has helped to create a culture in which we're not afraid to innovate or take risks. Our slightly unorthodox approach to the restaurant industry (such as opening our financial books to the entire company and getting everyone from dishwashers to senior managers involved in profit sharing) has attracted a diverse crew of smart and dedicated people, from a former attorney to a zoologist. We're so proud of and thankful for the motley crew and extended family that has joined us on our mission: making excellent food while also being mindful of our community and the planet.

That's the other part of what we do at Mei Mei. We strive to make food that not only tastes good, but also does good for the local and regional food system. We started our truck with a commitment to serve great local food and no factory farmed meat. We now source from more than fifty small farms and producers in the Northeast to support people and companies using natural, sustainable, and ethical methods. They put in some crazy hard work to make stellar ingredients like rooftop-grown arugula, heirloom breed pork, and traditionally stone-ground grains. We also choose lesser-known and underappreciated cuts of meat and varieties of fish, pay attention to seasonality, and utilize every edible part of a plant and animal.

We believe that if more people and more restaurants cooked this way, we'd have healthier bodies and a healthier food system.

We've written this book for the same reasons we opened our business: because we love to cook, eat, and feed people. We love to tell stories—through words and through meals—and we believe in the power of food to make connections, make people happy, and make a difference for our planet. We've learned a lot through running our businesses and hope this book—with recipes, professional advice, and shopping tips—can make delicious, sustainable cooking more accessible and achievable in your life as well.

That's what we mean by family style. Two little sisters and a big brother. The food-slinging, ass-kicking Mei Mei team. A community of our wonderful guests and regulars, farmers, chefs, cider makers, and donut bakers. And, now, you and your family as well. We've written these stories and recipes to bring our family love to you. We hope you enjoy.

COOKING AT HOME THE MEI MEI WAY

This book is filled with food we love to eat. We've designed these recipes to fit the way we buy and cook at our restaurant and at home. We try to be sustainable while keeping things affordable; we hope you'll find these guidelines useful if you're interested in doing the same. Here are the practices that govern our sourcing and cooking at Mei Mei:

1. Buy good meat.

2. Buy from people you know.

3. Buy food that's grown in season—but you don't always have to eat seasonally.

4. Eat food that's good for you and good for the soil.

5. Eat everything edible.

6. Buy and cook local food.

1. BUY GOOD MEAT.

Over years of talking to farmers and learning about food production, we've come to believe strongly in the importance of humanely raised meat. We urge you to buy the best meat you can afford, both when cooking at home and eating out. Putting your dollars toward good meat helps signal to chefs, restaurateurs, farmers, and grocery store buyers that more menu and shelf space should be devoted to sustainable meat production. And we've got some thoughts on how to make it more wallet-friendly too.

What exactly does "good meat" mean when it comes to food shopping? Vague labels are pervasive in both grocery stores and wholesale outlets. Many descriptions you see in the supermarket, such as free-range and all-natural, are more marketing terminology than true animal husbandry standards. Given the complexities of food labeling and regulation, it's no surprise that many people turn to organic food. However, while researching our options for organic meat, we came to feel that the terms *organic* and *free-range* are preferable but still don't guarantee all aspects of good husbandry or land stewardship. Instead, they reduce all-encompassing philosophies and learned wisdom into checklists to be met in exchange for a pricey marketing label. With that in mind, we chose the sourcing standard of *pasture-raised* meat for our businesses. To us, it means that the animals live as part of an ecosystem rather than a factory, during which they spend as much time outside as is safe and reasonable and are allowed to act on their instincts. They are cared for by people who prioritize natural farming over hormones and antibiotics, who consider the animals' quality of life as well as profit.

What does this all mean for you? We encourage you to educate yourself about animal husbandry and meat production. If you care about food, you should care about meat. Good meat costs more to produce, so we embrace underutilized and therefore cheaper cuts, buy in bulk, and sometimes we just eat less meat.

2. BUY FROM PEOPLE YOU KNOW.

We started our food truck with the goal of sourcing local food, but we were too small to work with a large-scale distributor. So we started the hunt for

New England vendors, dropping by farmers' markets and searching online for interesting artisan producers. Now we get grains from the L'Etoile family of Four Star Farms in Western Massachusetts and maple syrup from Bobo's Mountain Sugar, run by Irene's old environmental science teacher Tina and her husband, Skye, in Weston, Vermont. We buy produce from Allandale Farm, located a few miles from the restaurant, and pork from Irene's old bosses at The Piggery in Ithaca, New York. We're thankful for these wonderful relationships, and we love that our purchases help them grow their businesses, support their families, and keep money in our local economy.

The best part is that we met a lot of these producers by starting conversations at the farmers' market and getting in touch with friends of friends. This means you can do it too! Maybe you know someone who knows someone who farms or makes pickles or brews craft beer. Visit some local markets and talk to vendors. Ask them about their businesses and their stories. Search online for producers in your area and shoot them an e-mail. More than likely, they'll be psyched you got in touch and will happily help you figure out how to get their product.

3. BUY FOOD THAT'S GROWN IN SEASON— BUT YOU DON'T ALWAYS HAVE TO EAT SEASONALLY.

We always get excited about the arrival of fiddlehead ferns in the springtime and the glut of late summer tomatoes in August. As native New Englanders who yearn for an end to snow shoveling and icy streets every winter, we relish the changing of the seasons and the return of familiar plants like old friends. We love eating produce at its seasonal peak, like our favorite sweet corn, grown at Four Town Farm in Massachusetts. It's incredibly juicy and candy-sweet throughout the summer, so fresh we serve it raw. But what happens in the winter? With the right infrastructure—local commercial processors that get the corn off the cob, into tubs, and into the freezer—small farms like Four Town can store corn long after

the summer harvest and we can get exquisite sweet corn for fritters all year long. It's a large-scale version of what some of our grandparents used to do back in the day—pick produce at the peak of the season and put it up in jars for the wintertime. This way we can still enjoy the best of summer's bounty during the dark days of winter and support our local growers and processing facilities at the same time.

4. EAT FOOD THAT'S GOOD FOR YOU AND GOOD FOR THE SOIL.

Although we grew up eating a lot of plain white rice, we now cook with a lot of whole grains as well. Over the years, we've worked directly with New England farms that have introduced us to grains such as triticale, rye, and wheat berries. As we learned while talking to farmers and reading books like Dan Barber's *The Third Plate*, these types of grains can help enrich the soil and increase farmers' capacity to grow. Plus, they taste great and they're good for you, providing valuable nutrients in the bran and germ that are removed in refined grains like white rice and white flour. Consider swapping out your next bowl of rice for triticale, or try wheat berries instead of pasta for a more flavorful, nutritious version of classic dishes.

5. EAT EVERYTHING EDIBLE.

We hate throwing out food. At the same time, we love figuring out ways to use up leftover ingredients. Combing through the kitchen to create a meal is like playing a game—you win if you use up all the veggies in the crisper drawer, and you win again when you get to eat it! It's an effective way to save money and keeps good food out of the trash.

We also look for ways to use every edible part of every ingredient. We put kale stalks in our dumpling fillings and cilantro stems in our stocks. Chicken skin, broccoli leaves, and fish spines get turned into nightly specials and staff meals at the restaurant. You can do the same! Don't throw out a vegetable as soon as it starts to wilt—turn forgotten root vegetables into Quick

Pickled Carrots (page 24) or bake that leek into Cheddar Scallion Bread Pudding (page 113). Don't make decisions merely based on the looks of your vegetables and fruits—ugly or misshapen produce can still be tasty produce. And try planning your meals so leftovers can easily be repurposed into new dishes. We've included suggestions on how to use scraps and leftovers in lots of recipes.

6. BUY AND COOK LOCAL FOOD.

Although it's not an explicit part of our creative Chinese-American cuisine, we shape our menu around the bounty of our farmers and the wonderful seasonal products they grow in the Northeast. While local meats and vegetables are typically the stars of the show, we also use local supporting ingredients to broaden and enhance our cooking. We might look to Massachusetts cranberries instead of lemons for acidity, or Vermont maple syrup and Rhode Island honey instead of cane sugar for sweetness. Even basics like cooking oils can be found locally made; we discovered that cold-pressed Vermont-grown canola seeds make the richest, most flavorful canola oil, adding an unexpectedly luxurious feel to even the most basic vinaigrette. We love that these ingredients add more nuance to our food while celebrating our New England heritage and supporting our local food system. We encourage you to explore and cook with products made in your community by producers unique to your area. You may find that ingredients made near you—even basics like a locally ground flour—can be a delightful boost to your cooking.

SOME PRO TIPS
FROM OUR KITCHEN TO YOURS

People often assume that because we own a restaurant we're trained professional chefs and then they're scared to invite us over for dinner. Don't be! We're all self-trained cooks, albeit ones with some pro-level skills picked up since we started the business. Luckily, you don't have to put in a year on the food truck to add these lessons to your arsenal. So please read the tips below . . . and then invite us over for dinner, OK?

1. **Work clean!** We quickly learned the importance of an orderly workspace once we opened our food truck. If you don't keep your tiny workstation clean while you prep salads, plate sandwiches, and chop garnishes, chaos quickly ensues. Now, in our own kitchens, we consistently wipe down surfaces, put food scraps in waste bags (produce bags from the supermarket are perfect for this), and wash dishes as we go. Tidying while you work goes a long way; we find a cleaner kitchen makes for more relaxing and enjoyable cooking.

2. **Stay organized.** Our restaurant is stacked floor-to-ceiling with assorted containers, all labeled with Sharpies and blue painter's tape. We've adopted this organizing practice at home: quarts in our refrigerators hold prepped food, leftovers, and sauces; glass jars in the cupboard hold spices, grains, and more. Clear containers let you see what's inside, and blue tape labels help you identify that random brown substance in the freezer. And don't forget the date you made it, so you know exactly when it desperately needs to be thrown out.

3. **Embrace shortcuts.** We love cooking from scratch; we used to cure our own bacon and ferment our own kimchi. But we've come to appreciate ready-made items that make life easier, like superb bacon from our friends at The Piggery and kickass kimchi from Hawthorne Valley Farm. We lower our labor costs by incorporating preprocessed food—not the kind full of unpronounceable chemicals, but ingredients like cooked, peeled, and sliced beets that are ready to top

a salad. So, don't sweat it if you buy pre-sliced butternut squash or peeled garlic or frozen corn. We applaud the little tricks that help you cook, because we know firsthand that time-consuming tasks make you more likely to reach for the takeout menu.

4. Be prepared! When our food truck opens, all lunch ingredients have already been prepped and organized in what's called *mise en place*, French for "everything in its place." This is a key aspect of professional food service; we cook grains, mix dressings, and cut veggies beforehand so when your order comes in, your salad can be assembled in less than two minutes. The idea also applies to a lot of Chinese cooking; you'd better have all your components ready when you start to stir-fry, because woks cook fast! You can translate this to your kitchen by buying or preparing food ahead of time—say, during a leisurely weekend. Then, on nights when you get home late and need a fast meal, you can pull your ingredients out of the refrigerator and speedily get your dinner on the table, congratulating yourself all the while on cooking like a professional.

KITCHEN EQUIPMENT

Kitchen tools are fun, but the real workhorses of your kitchen are **a good knife and a solid cutting board.** A nice sharp chef's knife will make kitchen life much easier, safer, and more enjoyable than a dull knife that slips or forces you to saw aggressively through tough items. We like a big wooden board that won't move while chopping or mincing. If you have a lighter-weight board, place a wet dishcloth or paper towel underneath to help stabilize it.

The handy sidekick to your knife work is a **bench scraper**, also known as a dough cutter, for scooping up chopped food and transferring it to a pan. Don't

use your knife; it will dull the blade or, worse, slash your hand open. It's also helpful for portioning dough and cleaning—use it to scrape crumbs off a cutting board before wiping it down.

You can execute all our recipes with **a good skillet** (we love cast iron for its heat-retaining properties, but nonstick pans are also handy), **a medium saucepan**, and **a large pot** like a Dutch oven. We go through tons of **sheet pans** in the restaurant and recommend owning a couple half-size pans (baking sheets).

Woks are excellent for stir-frying, steaming, and deep-frying, but aren't the best option for many home kitchens. Our restaurant range blasts flames high enough to heat a wok on all sides, but most home stoves can't utilize a wok to such advantage. A flat pan typically offers more hot surface area to maximize crunch on fried rice or a noodle pancake. If you do purchase a wok, we recommend carbon steel, and you may need a special wok ring for stability on your stovetop.

Metal tongs act as heatproof robot hands for grabbing food out of hot water, flipping things in smoking pans, and countless other kitchen situations. **Silicone spatulas** are ideal for scraping pans and getting all the sauce out of a container. Also useful is a **spider** (a longer, wider version of a metal slotted spoon) for scooping food out of bubbling hot oil or water.

If tongs are robot hands, **chopsticks** are nimble robot fingers. Extra-long chopsticks live next to our stoves to pluck small items from hot pans or narrow containers, and they have the added benefit of two ends—one to use in the pan, and one to taste with (i.e., put in your mouth).

Buy oils and other sauces in bulk and store them in **squeeze bottles** for easy access and application—they'll help you work cleaner and save money. Stashed by the stove with a blue tape and Sharpie label, your favorite sauces will be at hand just when you need them, while the big expensive jug gets protected from heat and light degradation in the cupboard.

A **bamboo** or **metal steamer**, lined with sturdy leaves (like cabbage or collards) or parchment paper, gently cooks everything from veggies to whole fish. You can get the job done with a heatproof plate on a steamer rack (or even a few crumpled balls of aluminum foil), but the bamboo and metal versions typically are stackable, which allows you to steam on multiple levels. Plus, they're inexpensive at most Asian markets.

At the restaurant and food truck, we're required to have instant-read **thermometers** at all times to test for food safety. While a health inspector isn't going to show up in your kitchen, a good digital thermometer will help you cook meats exactly the way you want them, rather than poking at your steak and hoping for the best. Super-precise Thermapens are an excellent splurge purchase if you're into that sort of thing, but there are also reliable cheap versions that you can buy at any kitchen supply store or online for $10 to $20.

If you add only one thing to your repertoire, consider a **digital scale**—they are vastly more efficient and accurate than cup and spoon measurements. If you need convincing, take a look at our Cranberry Sweet and Sour Sauce recipe on page 15. With measuring cups and spoons, you'll need to use and wash seven different items; with a scale, only the bowl. A scale is also more precise, which is especially important when baking and when multiplying recipes.

Immersion blenders are super handy, easy to clean, and fit in very small spaces. You can use them to make soups, sauces, aiolis, and more.

A **mortar and pestle** (low-tech, more aesthetically pleasing) or a **spice grinder** (high-tech, fewer arm muscles required) will boost your kitchen game. Using whole spices instead of pre-ground ensures fresh and vibrant flavors. We like to use a small, inexpensive coffee grinder.

Last, a **Microplane** and a **mandoline**. Microplanes can grate ginger and garlic so fine that they're essentially a paste. Mandolines (we like the Japanese brand Benriner) will cut your vegetables into beautifully thin slices, making a simple dish look like a work of art.

PANTRY INGREDIENTS

Our pantries are well stocked with a diverse assortment of Asian ingredients, all useful for adding complexity and dimension to our cooking. Some we grew up eating, others we stumbled upon while exploring the endlessly stimulating aisles of our local Asian supermarkets. We've included our favorites here, ranging from basics like soy sauce to more unusual ingredients like fermented black beans. We love using these products to heighten flavor sensations, from brightening a soup with rice vinegar to enhancing the meaty richness of a stew with fish sauce. Try adding some to your pantry; stocked with these building blocks, you'll be able to transform the simplest of dishes—from steamed vegetables to scrambled eggs to boiled noodles—into a compelling and satisfying meal.

BASIC ASIAN PANTRY
Most of these items can be found in mainstream grocery stores.

Chili garlic sauce—Similar to sambal oelek, this spicy garlicky red sauce with lots of yummy bits will keep in your fridge for ages; spoon it on everything from soup to rice to eggs to noodles.

Coconut milk—Coconut milk has a rich sweetness and makes a delightfully creamy dairy substitute. We prefer the unsweetened, full-fat version and keep many cans of Chaokoh brand stacked in our cupboards.

Fish sauce—We love that this pungent salted anchovy sauce used to be an obscure Asian ingredient and now can be found in our local supermarket. We like Squid brand as a basic option, but try Red Boat if you want to get a bit fancier.

Hoisin sauce—A thick, sweet sauce, traditionally made from fermented soybeans, somewhat similar to an American barbecue sauce. We make our own with apples and sweet potatoes (page 16), but the store-bought versions generally are very good, if sometimes quite sugary.

Kimchi—We've found an impressive selection of this fermented vegetable condiment in mainstream supermarkets. The most common Korean version is made with napa cabbage, but additional flavors and vegetables are springing up everywhere from Asian grocers to natural foods stores. Our favorite is from Hawthorne Valley Farm. A scoop will add kick to noodles, salads, curries, sandwiches, and more.

Miso paste—This salty fermented soybean paste adds an umami boost to savory as well as sweet dishes (sounds weird, but try it in our Miso Sesame Chocolate Chip Cookies (page 227) and you'll be converted too). Most are made with rice, but some include barley or other grains, so check the ingredients if you're cooking gluten-free. We typically use subtly flavored white miso, but if you purchase a selection, the little tubs will keep in your refrigerator for months.

Oyster sauce—This sauce can add a funky, flavorful boost to many Asian dishes. The taste varies quite a bit by brand—some are sweeter, some are intense and bitter, so make sure to taste and adjust the seasoning to your preference.

Panko—These light and puffy Japanese breadcrumbs offer an unrivaled crunch. Toast some with a bit of garlic (page 14) and sprinkle it on everything you eat.

Rice and noodles—There are innumerable varieties and styles of Asian noodles and rice—we encourage you to try them all and discover your favorites. Since each could have its own cookbook and still barely scratch the surface, we've only included the ones we use most often here.

Dried rice noodles—Sometimes called rice sticks, you'll recognize these lightly translucent noodles of roughly linguini width as the ubiquitous pad thai noodle.

Fresh or frozen ramen—While you can always steal a brick of freeze-dried ramen from an instant noodle package, fresh ramen (usually found frozen) is definitely worth seeking out. We like Sun brand, used by many famous ramen shops and available at a growing number of stores around the country.

Jasmine rice—We like this lightly fragrant long-grain rice in both sweet and savory dishes. The individual grains stay a bit more separate than with medium-grain rice, which can be helpful when cooking fried rice.

Medium-grain white rice—This simple, affordable white rice is the everyday rice of both our home and the restaurant. Sometimes short-grain rice is interchangeable; other times it's specifically meant for sushi, so check the package for more information.

Shanxi noodles—These flat white wheat noodles (a wider, fettuccine equivalent) can be found fresh or dried. Their plain taste and hearty texture make them versatile for many different dishes—boil to eat with a simple sauce, drain and toss in a hot oiled pan for a stir-fried noodle dish, or add to hot broth for a hearty soup.

Soba noodles—These buckwheat noodles are nutty and toothsome. They're excellent served hot but are sturdy enough for cold dishes.

Rice vinegar—When we're looking for an acidic component in our cooking, we reach for rice vinegar (sometimes labeled rice wine vinegar). Our go-to is Marukan unseasoned rice vinegar; the seasoned version can be good for quick pickles and dressings.

Seaweed—There's a whole exciting world of seaweeds and edible ocean plants out there. Here are the three we use most often:

Sichuan peppercorns

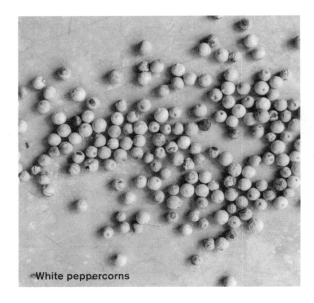

White peppercorns

Kombu—The most substantial of these three seaweeds, this dried kelp comes in hardened sheets and needs to be simmered or steeped (not boiled) into an umami broth. Along with katsuobushi (see page 9), the two make the Japanese soup stock called dashi that forms the base of many savory dishes.

Nori—The flat roasted sheets of seaweed that wrap most sushi rolls. The salted strips are an addictive snack on their own in that can't-eat-just-one potato chip kind of way.

Wakame—These dried seaweed flakes have a brinier, more ocean-y flavor than nori and need to be quickly hydrated in cold water before using.

Sesame oil, toasted—With a splash of soy sauce and sesame oil, you can make a delectable sauce in seconds. Look for a pure toasted oil, which will be dark in color and rich in flavor. Our favorite brand, Kadoya, and most other Asian brands aren't labeled as toasted, but you'll know from the color. Use only untoasted sesame oil for cooking, as the toasted oil has a low smoke point and therefore can't be brought to a super high heat.

Soy sauce—There are countless types of soy sauce out there; a basic light soy sauce will work for all our recipes (*light* refers to color and consistency, not sodium content). If you're looking to minimize your salt intake or want more control over salt levels in your cooking, we are partial to Kikkoman Less Sodium in the green bottle. It's also nice to have tamari or gluten-free soy sauce on hand.

Sriracha—We've always got bottles of Huy Fong rooster sauce around, but many small companies are now making excellent artisanal chili sauce. Our friends at Kitchen Garden in Sutherland, Massachusetts, make a super fruity habanero sriracha that will knock your socks off.

ADVANCED ASIAN PANTRY
These less common ingredients may require a special trip to an Asian market or an online order, but all offer exciting and intriguing flavor profiles. From the funk of doubanjiang to the tingle of Sichuan peppercorns, these sauces, pastes, and spices will add layer upon layer of flavor to elevate your cooking.

Black vinegar (sometimes labeled Chinkiang or Zhenjiang vinegar)—This dark aged vinegar is key to

Fermented black beans

Star anise

a good dumpling dip, but also adds depth to cooked dishes. Black vinegar is made from glutinous rice and typically includes wheat, so substitute with rice or balsamic vinegar to make a recipe gluten-free. We typically buy the Gold Plum brand with the yellow label and cap.

Bonito flakes or katsuobushi—This distinctive Japanese ingredient is made from a complex process involving the gutting, filleting, simmering, smoking, drying, and fermenting of a bonito fish or a skipjack tuna. Whew! The production can take months or even years and results in dried fish as hard as wood, which is then shaved into pinkish-brown flakes. These flakes are combined with kombu seaweed (see page 8) to create dashi broth or used as a topping for many Japanese dishes.

Chinese sesame paste—Typically made from roasted white sesame seeds, but there are many varieties with different flavor profiles. Try to find a paste labeled *pure*. It's similar enough to tahini that you can use them interchangeably in our recipes.

Curry paste—These Southeast Asian blends of spices and aromatics (anything from lemongrass to ginger to hot peppers) will save you boatloads of shopping and

chopping time, making curry a reasonable weeknight effort rather than a daylong project. We like Maesri brand, which comes in a rainbow of colors, flavors, and sizes ranging from small packets to medium cans to enormous tubs. Check the label if you're vegetarian, as some varieties or brands contain shrimp.

Doubanjiang (sometimes labeled as toban djan, broad bean chili sauce, or Sichuan hot bean paste)—This thick, spicy dark red paste is made from fermented broad beans, also known as fava beans, and chilies. It's rich, salty, and funky. It can contain wheat flour, so substitute chili garlic sauce or another fermented chili paste if you're cooking gluten-free.

Fermented black beans—Sometimes labeled salted or preserved black beans, these aren't black beans like you'd eat in a burrito, but are actually soybeans fermented without liquid. These little guys add a crazy amount of umami flavor to your cooking and typically come in a clear plastic bag; transfer them to an airtight jar to prevent spoilage (and contain their particularly distinct fragrance). Sift out any sticks or rocks and rinse in cold water before using. Soak longer, up to overnight, to remove even more salt.

Five-spice powder—This classic Chinese spice blend

varies slightly by preparation, but typically includes star anise, Sichuan peppercorns, cloves, fennel, and cinnamon, although cassia bark and/or ginger sometimes make an appearance. Buy it as a powder for ease, or grind your own to customize the blend and ensure peak freshness or make a cool homemade gift.

Gochujang—This Korean red pepper paste/sauce is made from gochugaru (gochu = chile pepper, garu = flakes or powder). It's great to have in your fridge to add depth and a hit of spice to any number of savory sauces.

Shaoxing wine—This amber-hued rice wine (sometimes labeled Shao hsing) is specifically made for cooking. Many old-school cookbooks recommend sherry as a substitute, but it's easier to keep an inexpensive bottle of Shaoxing wine in your cupboard than a pricier bottle of sherry in your fridge, so why not get the real thing? It adds a depth and subtle sweetness to savory dishes, often with notes of vanilla and other warm spices.

Sichuan peppercorns—Unlike black or white peppercorns, these aren't actually related to the pepper family but are the seeds of the prickly ash tree (which is sometimes how you will find them labeled). They're not exactly spicy, but instead provide a fascinating tingly-numbing sensation unlike anything else out there.

Star anise—This dried brown eight-pointed seedpod adds a licorice note to braises and sauces and makes for a nice decorative addition to a jar of pickles.

White pepper—An earthier, more floral version of black pepper. Both are the fruit of the pepper plant, but white peppercorns have the sun-dried outer husk removed.

CHINESE AROMATICS, AKA THE CHINESE TRINITY

The dishes of many cuisines around the world begin with a base of three aromatic vegetables, from the French *mirepoix* of onion, carrot, and celery to the Cajun and Creole holy trinity of onion, celery, and green bell pepper. Ginger, garlic, and scallions are the essential trio of Chinese cooking, and we always keep them stocked in the kitchen.

Ginger: Look for big, unwrinkled "hands" of ginger and store them in the refrigerator for up to a few weeks. You can also freeze ginger; it softens upon defrosting, but maintains its distinct flavor. If you are peeling a knobby piece, the least wasteful method is to scrape the skin with the edge of a spoon. The fastest method is to slice off the skin and any stubby bits with a sharp knife.

Garlic: We start nearly every recipe by smashing a garlic clove against the edge of a large chef's knife. Smashing effortlessly removes the outer husk, and the clove is easier to mince once it's slightly flattened. Use a smashed whole clove when you want the released garlic flavor but not all the little bits, like in dipping sauces. Keep garlic heads intact as long as you can and store them somewhere cool and dark. If you buy peeled garlic, store it in the fridge.

Scallions: In Chinese cooking, you use the whole scallion—don't throw out the dark green parts! Trim off the hairy roots, and the dark green tips if you are using the greens for garnish. If your scallions have been lingering, pull off any yellowing stalks or slimy outer layers before use. Even if they've gone a bit limp, you can still use them in recipes like Ginger Scallion Oil (page 101) and Cheddar Scallion Bread Pudding (page 113).

A SPECIAL NOTE ON SALT

Properly seasoning a dish with salt can be challenging, but it's an essential aspect of cooking well. Too little salt and a dish will taste flat and bland; salt punches up the flavor of even the subtlest ingredients. Too much salt and your dish will be painfully inedible. You'll want to find the right balance for you and the people you cook for, as well as understanding the salt you have in your kitchen and how it tastes. We sometimes struggle with this at home; Irene likes an assertively, generously seasoned meal, while our mom, with her high blood pressure, prefers dishes to be lightly seasoned or even unsalted. Sometimes she's horrified when Irene grabs a full five-fingered pinch of salt and casually tosses it over a salad, but we'd argue that's exactly why the greens taste so good.

We always use kosher salt while cooking (the Diamond Crystal brand) instead of iodized table salt for a cleaner, purer taste. You'll notice that sometimes we include specific amounts of salt in recipes (use about half as much if you're using Morton kosher salt or table salt), other times we specify to taste for seasoning, and sometimes we do both. It's impossible to say exactly how much salt a dish should have, both because it's a matter of personal preference and because saltiness will vary depending on ingredients and brands. Some dishes feature naturally salty ingredients like miso or fermented black beans. Others you may need to salt well in order to maximize flavor. It's really up to you. No matter your preferences, make sure you season and taste throughout the cooking process. Once dinner is on the table, we use a flaky sea salt by Maldon or our friends at Atlantic Saltworks for a bit of texture and a last hit of flavor.

A Note on Dietary Restrictions from Andy

When I first began formal restaurant management training, I was lucky enough to work for a company that set the standard for allergen awareness training. Allergies were taken very seriously; violation of policy was grounds for immediate termination!

However, it wasn't until I became a father that I realized how important it was to be educated and knowledgeable on the topic of food allergies. I've seen allergic reactions to everything from a Tootsie Roll (milk protein) to a gummy worm (wheat). I know it's serious because my son would never willingly spit out any candy unless it was an emergency!

We appreciate that guests come to our restaurants because they feel comfortable telling us what they need, and they know we'll address the issue properly. We hope to be as helpful and informative in this book, to help you cook for yourself and your loved ones safely and enjoyably.

Throughout the book, these abbreviations are used to help you find dishes that best suit your dietary needs. When "O" is used after any of the abbreviations, it means "optional."

DF	Dairy Free
GF	Gluten Free
V	Vegetarian
VV	Vegan

OUR FAVORITE PANTRY RECIPES

These sauces, starches, oils, and garnishes are our go-to recipes for adding texture, balance, and variety to many a simple meal. With these recipes in your repertoire, you'll be able to quickly stir together a sauce to accompany a stir-fry or pickle veggies to enliven a salad or noodles. If you've got some time on your hands, make an aioli, infuse some oil, or fry some shallots for sprinkling. The next time you're trying to put together a quick dish, you'll be delighted to find these versatile, tried-and-true items ready to amp up your meal.

WHITE RICE

———— V, VV, GF, DF ————

We grew up with a rice cooker, but these days we just use this stovetop method to make plain white rice (short-, medium-, or long-grain) with just a pan and a lid. Rinse the rice to wash away the starch if you're planning on making fried rice; don't bother if you're making Rice Cakes (page 42) or you don't feel like it.

Makes 3 cups

1½ cups (360 g) water	1 cup (185 g) white rice

Put the rice and water in a medium heavy-bottomed saucepan for which you have a lid. Stir the rice to remove any clumps, then bring the water to a boil over medium-high heat. Stir again, then turn the heat down to low and cover the pot. Cook for 15 minutes, then check the rice; give it another minute or so if it is undercooked. Turn off the heat, fluff up the rice with your spatula, then cover and let sit for 10 minutes before serving.

GARLIC PANKO

———— V, VV, DF ————

Makes ½ cup

2 tablespoons (26 g) neutral oil or olive oil	½ cup (40 g) Japanese panko or homemade breadcrumbs
1 clove garlic	Pinch of kosher salt

Heat the oil in a medium skillet over medium-low heat until shimmering, then add the garlic and stir until lightly browned, about 1 minute. Add the panko and cook, stirring constantly, until the breadcrumbs darken to a deep golden brown, about 3 minutes. Discard the garlic clove, transfer to a plate, sprinkle with the salt, and set aside to cool. Store in an airtight container at room temperature for up to 2 weeks.

SOY VINEGAR DIPPING SAUCE

—— V, VV, GFO, DF ——

Consider this basic dumpling sauce a starting point for the sauce of your dreams. Our mom, who eats a low-sodium diet, leaves out the soy sauce in favor of some water and a pinch of sugar. If you have very fatty, meaty dumplings, try increasing the amount of black vinegar. If you like it spicy, add in more chili sauce or sriracha or the hot sauce of your choice.

Makes 1 cup

½ cup (120 g) soy sauce (substitute tamari if gluten-free)

⅓ cup (80 g) black vinegar (substitute rice vinegar if unavailable or if gluten-free)

¼ cup (15 g) chopped scallions

1 clove garlic, smashed

1 teaspoon (5 g) chili sauce or hot sauce

1 teaspoon (4 g) toasted sesame oil

Whisk together all the ingredients in a bowl. Store in an airtight container in the refrigerator for up to 2 weeks.

CRANBERRY SWEET AND SOUR SAUCE

—— V, VV, GF, DF ——

This vivid and tangy sauce is a stellar companion to Dim Sum Turnip Cakes (page 41), Salt and Pepper Chicken Wings (page 157), and Farmers' Market Fried Rice (page 119), among many other dishes.

Makes 2 cups

1¼ cups (5 ounces/ 140 g) frozen cranberries

½ cup (120 g) water

½ cup (100 g) sugar

⅓ cup (80 g) rice vinegar

¼ cup (60 g) red wine vinegar

¼ cup (30 g) minced onion

3 tablespoons (45 g) tomato paste

2 teaspoons (6 g) kosher salt

2 cloves garlic, minced

½ teaspoon (2 g) celery salt

Pinch of ground cloves

Combine all the ingredients in a medium saucepan and bring to a boil over medium heat. Reduce the heat slightly and simmer for 10 minutes. Remove from the heat and let cool completely. Transfer to a blender (or use an immersion blender) and blend until smooth. Store in a covered container in the refrigerator for up to 1 month.

APPLE HOISIN SAUCE

—— V, VV, GF, DF ——

This untraditional hoisin recipe created by our opening co-chef Max Hull features an unlikely list of ingredients (unless you have a baby at home, in which case mashed sweet potato and applesauce are basically kitchen essentials). However, we'd venture that this sweet and funky take on hoisin is worth the effort.

Makes 2 cups

1 cup (240 g) water

¾ cup (150 g) sugar

⅔ cup (175 g) applesauce

½ cup (110 g) cooked mashed sweet potato

⅓ cup (50 g) fermented black beans, rinsed

6 cloves garlic

2 tablespoons (30 g) apple cider vinegar

1 tablespoon (20 g) molasses

1 tablespoon (15 g) balsamic vinegar

1½ teaspoons (5 g) kosher salt

1 teaspoon (2 g) five-spice powder

Pinch of chili flakes or cayenne

Combine all the ingredients in a blender and blend until smooth. Transfer to a medium saucepan and bring to a boil over medium-high heat. Reduce the heat to medium-low and simmer until thick, 10 to 15 minutes. Let cool, then store in a covered container in the fridge for up to 1 month.

SOY GINGER DRESSING

—— V, VV, GFO, DF ——

Makes 1 cup

½ cup (105 g) neutral oil, such as canola

¼ cup (60 g) rice vinegar

3 tablespoons (40 g) toasted sesame oil

One 1-inch piece fresh ginger, minced

1½ tablespoons (30 g) maple syrup

1½ tablespoons (22 g) soy sauce (substitute tamari if gluten-free)

1 teaspoon (5 g) Dijon mustard

Put all the ingredients in a bowl, blender, or food processor and whisk or blend to combine. Store in an airtight container in the fridge for up to 3 weeks.

MISO HONEY DRESSING

—— V, GF, DF ——

Makes 1 cup

2 cloves garlic, sliced

¾ cup (157 g) neutral oil

¼ cup (60 g) rice vinegar

1 tablespoon (17 g) miso paste

2 teaspoons (14 g) honey

Kosher salt

Place the garlic in a small skillet. Place over high heat and cook until lightly charred, about 3 minutes, then flip and lightly char the other side. Remove from heat, let cool, then mince. Combine the oil, vinegar, miso, and honey in a bowl and whisk to dissolve the miso and honey. Add the garlic and mix thoroughly, then season with salt. Store in an airtight container in the refrigerator for up to 2 weeks.

FERMENTED BLACK BEAN DRESSING

—— V, VV, GF, DF ——

An umami-rich dressing, delicious on salads, cold noodles, and more.

Makes 1 cup

½ cup (105 g) neutral oil, such as canola

¼ cup (60 g) rice vinegar

¼ cup (52 g) extra-virgin olive oil

1 tablespoon (10 g) fermented black beans, rinsed

2 teaspoons (8 g) brown sugar

Kosher salt

Combine all the ingredients in a blender and blend until smooth. Season to taste, then store in an airtight container in the refrigerator for up to 2 weeks.

PEANUT SAUCE

—— V, VV, GFO, DF ——

I could eat this sauce on noodles, salads, grilled meats, or roasted veggies every day. Consider adding sriracha, minced garlic or ginger, swapping the vinegar for lime juice, or customizing as you see fit.

Makes ½ cup

3 tablespoons (45 g) unsweetened, creamy peanut butter

2 tablespoons (30 g) soy sauce (substitute tamari if gluten-free)

1½ tablespoons (22 g) rice vinegar

1 tablespoon (15 g) water

1 teaspoon (4 g) toasted sesame oil

Put all the ingredients in a small bowl and whisk to combine. Taste and adjust the seasonings, keeping in mind the sauce will vary according to your brands of peanut butter and soy sauce. Tinker with the amounts to achieve your preferred flavor and consistency. Store in an airtight container in the refrigerator for up to 2 weeks.

GINGER SCALLION OIL

—— V, VV, GF, DF ——

You may recognize ginger scallion oil, or GSO as we affectionately call it, as the magical Chinese restaurant concoction that makes just about everything taste better. Chicken, noodles, and rice are classic companions, but less typical Chinese ingredients can also be upgraded with a spoonful or five (try mixing some into ricotta cheese for one of our go-to dips). Back in the day, we'd heat oil by the gallon and, clad in protective goggles and oven mitts, trudge outside to pour it over the aromatics and watch steam and sparks shoot five feet into the air. Thankfully, this smaller-scale stovetop method is less likely to singe your eyebrows off.

Makes ¾ cup

½ cup neutral oil (105 g), such as grapeseed or peanut

1 bunch scallions, minced (about 1¼ cups/65 g)

¼ cup (40 g) finely minced fresh ginger

Kosher salt

Heat the oil in a large pot over high heat until it begins to smoke (about 395°F/200°C). Standing back, quickly add the scallions and ginger. Remove from heat and stir to coat all the ginger and scallion bits. Salt to taste.

Let cool completely, store in a sealed container in the refrigerator, and spoon onto anything from scrambled eggs to avocado toast. It will keep for 1 to 2 weeks, although mine never lasts that long.

CHILI OIL

—— V, VV, GF, DF ——

Makes 1 cup

1 cup (210 g) neutral oil such as canola	2 tablespoons (8 g) Sichuan peppercorns
One 1-inch piece fresh ginger, sliced	½ cup (40 g) chili flakes
2 cloves garlic, sliced	Kosher salt
2 star anise	

Combine the oil, ginger, garlic, star anise, and Sichuan peppercorns in a small saucepan and heat over medium-high heat until sizzling. Reduce the heat to low and cook for 10 minutes. Put the chili flakes into a heatproof container with some extra room, then carefully strain the hot oil into the container. Discard the ginger, garlic, and spices, let the oil cool, then stir and season with salt. Store in an airtight container in the refrigerator for up to 2 weeks.

TOASTED SALT AND PEPPERCORNS

—— V, VV, GF, DF ——

We have fond memories of this dry-fried spice blend sitting on banquet tables whenever we went out to dinner with our Grandma Li. Store some by the stove for seasoning everything from meat to fish to veggies. Store the rest in your pantry in an airtight container for ages. Package it into cute little jars, and give to your favorite people. The amounts and types of peppercorns are up to you—we like a heavy dose of Sichuan peppercorns against a backdrop of white and black pepper—but feel free to experiment.

Makes about ⅓ cup

¼ cup (40 g) kosher salt	1 tablespoon (8 g) black peppercorns
¼ cup (16 g) Sichuan peppercorns	1 tablespoon (8 g) white peppercorns

Combine all the ingredients in a medium skillet over medium-low heat. Toast until the peppercorns start to make a popping sound in the pan and let off wafts of smoke, about 10 to 15 minutes. Let cool, then grind in a mortar and pestle or spice grinder.

FRIED SHALLOTS

—— V, VV, GF, DF ——

Along with Garlic Panko (page 14) and peanuts, fried shallots are our go-to garnish when we want more crunch.

Makes 1 cup

4 shallots

Neutral oil, such as canola, for frying

Kosher salt

Peel and thinly slice the shallots using a sharp knife or mandoline. Using your hands, separate the shallot slices into rings. Line a plate with paper towels.

Pour the oil into a medium heavy-bottomed saucepan to a depth of 1 inch. Heat to 300°F (150°C) over medium-high heat, then, using a spider or slotted spoon, carefully add the shallots. Fry, stirring occasionally, until the shallots are mostly golden brown, about 5 minutes.

Use the spider or slotted spoon to remove the shallots from the oil and place on the prepared plate. Immediately sprinkle with a good-size pinch of salt and let cool. If not eating right away, store in a sealed container at room temperature for up to 1 week, although we doubt they'll last that long.

HONEY WALNUT MAYONNAISE

—— V, GF, DF ——

Makes 1 cup

1 large egg yolk

1 tablespoon (15 g) rice vinegar

¼ teaspoon (1 g) kosher salt

¾ cup (157 g) walnut oil

1½ tablespoons (30 g) honey, or to taste

Put the egg yolk, vinegar, and salt in a sturdy medium bowl and whisk to combine. If your bowl keeps sliding around, place it on top of a damp paper towel.

Very slowly, drip the oil into the bowl (we recommend a spouted container or squeeze bottle), starting with a drop at a time and whisking vigorously as you pour. It will seem very, very slow, but if you get too impatient and speed up, you may end up breaking the mayonnaise. Once the mixture is thickened and well emulsified (thoroughly blended), after about half of the oil has been added, pour at a faster rate and whisk in the remaining oil. Whisk in the honey.

SRIRACHA AIOLI AND SOY AIOLI

Sometimes we think Mei Mei exists only to provide food that you can use to shovel aioli into your mouth. People ask for extra helpings of these aiolis all the time; they're worth all the whisking, trust us, and can live in a sealed container in the refrigerator for up to one week for all your dipping needs.

However, we prefer to avoid all that whisking and use our favorite mayonnaise tool: an immersion blender. Put the starter ingredients into a tall, narrow container and whizz to combine, then add the oil in a slow stream. Every so often, stop pouring to slowly move the blender up and down and incorporate the oil as it pools on top. The consistency will be thicker than if you whisked; add a little water at the end if you want to thin it out or more soy sauce or vinegar to adjust the flavor.

DOUBLE AWESOME CHINESE FOOD

SRIRACHA AIOLI

V, GF, DF

Makes 1 cup

1 large egg yolk

2 cloves garlic, finely minced or grated on a Microplane

2 tablespoons (30 g) sriracha

1½ tablespoons (22 g) rice vinegar

¼ teaspoon (1 g) kosher salt, or to taste

¼ teaspoon (1 g) sugar, or to taste

¾ cup (157 g) neutral oil, such as canola

Put the egg yolk, garlic, 1 tablespoon of the sriracha, 1 tablespoon of the rice vinegar, the salt, and sugar in a sturdy medium bowl and whisk to combine. If your bowl keeps sliding around, place it on top of a damp paper towel.

Very slowly, drip the oil into the bowl (we recommend a spouted container or squeeze bottle), starting with a drop at a time and whisking vigorously as you pour. It will seem very, very slow, but if you get too impatient and speed up, you may end up breaking the mayonnaise. Once the mixture is thickened and well emulsified (thoroughly blended), after about half of the oil has been added, pour at a faster rate and whisk in the remaining oil. Whisk in the remaining 1 tablespoon sriracha and ½ tablespoon rice vinegar. Taste and whisk in more salt or sugar, if desired.

SOY AIOLI

V, GFO, DF

Makes 1 cup

1 large egg yolk

2 cloves garlic, finely minced or grated on a Microplane

2 tablespoons (30 g) soy sauce (substitute tamari if gluten-free)

1½ tablespoons (22 g) rice vinegar

¾ cup (157 g) neutral oil, such as canola

Put the egg yolk, garlic, 1½ tablespoons of the soy sauce, and 1 tablespoon of the rice vinegar in a sturdy medium bowl and whisk to combine. If your bowl keeps sliding around, place it on top of a damp paper towel.

Very slowly, drip the oil into the bowl (we recommend a spouted container or squeeze bottle), starting with a drop at a time and whisking vigorously as you pour. It will seem very, very slow, but if you get too impatient and speed up, you may end up breaking the mayonnaise. Once the mixture is thickened and well emulsified (thoroughly blended), after about half of the oil has been added, pour at a faster rate and whisk in the remaining oil. Whisk in the remaining ½ tablespoon soy sauce and ½ tablespoon vinegar.

PICKLED CRANBERRIES

—— V, VV, GF, DF ——

These chubby little bursts of sweet and sour will add a big kick of flavor to salads, grains, yogurt, and more.

Makes 1 cup

⅔ cup (160 g) rice vinegar

⅓ cup (80 g) very hot water

2 tablespoons (25 g) sugar

1½ teaspoons (5 g) kosher salt

1 cup (150 g) dried, unsweetened cranberries

Put the vinegar, water, sugar, and salt in a small bowl or pint jar and stir to dissolve the salt and sugar. Add the cranberries and let sit for at least 1 hour in the refrigerator before using. Store in an airtight container in the refrigerator for up to one month.

QUICK PICKLED CARROTS

—— V, VV GF, DF ——

This carrot-ginger combo can lightly pickle in the amount of time it takes you to stir-fry some meat and boil noodles, perfect for a nice crunchy last-minute flavor boost. Try the basic brine with just about any thinly sliced vegetable, such as radishes, cucumbers, or shallots.

Makes 2 cups

1 cup (240 g) very hot water

1 cup (240 g) rice vinegar

2 tablespoons (25 g) sugar

2 tablespoons (20 g) kosher salt

3 medium carrots, thinly sliced

One 1-inch piece fresh ginger, peeled and thinly sliced into matchsticks

Combine the water, vinegar, sugar, and salt in a large bowl and stir to dissolve the salt and sugar. Add the carrots and ginger and let cool. Drain any pickles you want to eat right away, then seal the remainder in an airtight container and store in the refrigerator for up to two weeks.

CABBAGE PICKLES
(OR, NOT-AS-QUICK PICKLES)

—— V, VV GF, DF ——

We love the color and bite of these bright pink cabbage pickles at the restaurant, but try just about any other vegetable (and any spices or aromatics) for a slower take on pickled veggies.

Makes 2 cups

1¼ cups (300 g) water

1 cup (240 g) apple cider vinegar

1 cup (240 g) rice vinegar

¾ cup (150 g) sugar

1½ tablespoons (15 g) kosher salt

One 1-inch piece fresh ginger, sliced

A few onion scraps, such as the top and bottom of an onion

1 teaspoon (4 g) caraway seeds

1 teaspoon (4 g) black peppercorns

½ teaspoon (2 g) whole mustard seeds

3 whole cloves

1 bay leaf

3 cups thinly sliced red cabbage (about ½ small cabbage/ 9 ounces/250 g)

Combine all the ingredients except the cabbage in a medium saucepan and bring to boil. Reduce the heat to very low and cook for 30 minutes. Put the cabbage in a large heatproof container and immediately strain the hot liquid over the cabbage. Discard the spices and scraps. Let cool, then seal and keep in the refrigerator for up to 2 weeks.

CHINESE CLASSICS THE MEI MEI WAY

We're often asked if our recipes are based on dishes that our mother cooked for us growing up. Perhaps they imagine a hardworking Chinese mom, toiling away in a kitchen full of steamer baskets and fragrantly bubbling pots. Picture this instead: a doctor of internal medicine who was born in Boston and knows more about the New England Patriots defensive line than how to roast a duck. With Mom seeing patients full-time and Dad doing groundbreaking cancer research, getting food on the table and taking care of us kids was handled by a series of babysitters. Food was important—and being home in time for dinner was especially important—but because meals were valuable family time, not because of any gourmet sensibilities or culinary obsessions.

Our Grandma Li, on the other hand, was deeply involved in food, but she didn't hand down generations-old family recipes or teach us to make noodles. Our father's mother, Chu Fang Li, ran China Garden, considered one of the best Chinese restaurants north of New York City from the mid-1950s to the mid-1970s. She was a total badass. And she didn't actually cook—she ordered the cooks around while dressed in a sheath of Chinese silk. In a grand dining room filled with embroidered tapestries and jade sculptures, she told you what specialties to order, what seafood was the freshest that day, which Chinese delicacy you absolutely had to try. She was a natural hostess and a local celebrity, appearing on TV game shows and getting profiled in endless newspapers and magazines. She was, as *Gotham Guide* called her, a "dynamic, indefatigable, utterly charming lady boss."

Although Grandma celebrated the history and artistry of gourmet Chinese cuisine and enjoyed introducing it to American diners, she encouraged her children to pursue higher education over following her into the restaurant business. So while our mom and dad loved and appreciated good food (we've heard Dad carried soy sauce around in his doctor's bag during medical school), we had many other influences shaping the food we ate growing up. Dinner was often a mix of home-style Chinese dishes, 1980s American brands, and, always, white rice. We didn't think of it as particularly Chinese. Funny enough, the only dish we called Chinese as kids wasn't even Chinese at all. Chinese noodles was the name our parents gave to Japanese instant ramen, which was as much a staple in our home as American classics like boxed spaghetti, Pop-Tarts, and Fruit Roll-Ups. The parade of babysitters did a lot more to fuel our appetites and expose us to new dishes, from far-flung locales like France, Spain, Iceland, and Minnesota, all equally different and exotic to us kids. With Florence from France, we gamely sampled coq au vin and made gross-out faces at the weird vegetable dish called

ratatouille. With Lisa of Minnesota, we meticulously sliced apples for towering pies doused in cinnamon and sugar and carefully layered ground beef and mashed potatoes for shepherd's pie.

And then there were all the Chinese babysitters: Auntie Yan Hua, Chun Han, Jie Lan, Ai Guo, and Shi Hui, to name just a few. Each brought his or her own specialties and cherished dishes from a different region of China, so we were introduced to a wide range of humble home-cooked meals. A bowl of Rice Porridge (page 31) epitomizes this warmth and simplicity of our childhood eating. At restaurants in Boston's Chinatown, we got exposed to more complex gourmet dishes like Peking duck and dim sum classics. We've included a recipe for our father's beloved Dim Sum Turnip Cake (page 41), which has been a popular item made with local farm produce at our restaurant. And we can't forget

our neighborhood Americanized Chinese restaurant, a neon-lit, linoleum-covered takeout spot called Dragon Star; there will always be places in our hearts for the Chinese takeout standards. Hence, we've got recipes for Beef and Broccoli (page 34) and Cranberry Sweet and Sour Stir-Fried Pork (page 42) but with unexpected twists and local ingredients to boost the flavors and textures of these nostalgic dishes.

These childhood memories, interwoven with diverse ideas and interpretations of Chinese food in America, have influenced the way we cook at Mei Mei and the way we eat at home. In creating these recipes, we started with our love and nostalgia for classic Chinese dishes, added some of our favorite tips and techniques, and tossed in some seasonal New England ingredients. We hope the resulting dishes become classics for your family too.

RICE PORRIDGE THREE WAYS
(AKA XI FAN, OR CONGEE, OR JOOK)

In our house, *xi fan* was the equivalent of chicken noodle or matzo ball soup—the Chinese grandma's version of Jewish penicillin. We'd slurp this cozy, filling rice porridge, also known as jook or congee, when sick in bed, upset, or otherwise needing a big bowl of comfort.

We've included three versions, each one perfect for huddling over a bowl on your own or placing a big pot on the table with an array of toppings for friends and family. Each serves four or more, with Toppings (page 33).

SIMPLE RICE PORRIDGE

——— V, VV, GF, DF ———

This xi fan is the kind we grew up eating—ideal for cooking on a budget and cold winter nights. It's great for kids, with a texture perfect for the youngest of eaters and the fun of designing your own bowl. We also appreciate a meal that can be made with a minimum of effort—combine the rice and water and just simmer away while you gather your toppings of choice.

1 cup (185 g) white rice   Kosher salt

10 cups (2.4 kg) water
(or broth or stock)

Combine the rice and water in a large pot over medium-high heat. No need to wash the rice; the additional starch will help thicken the porridge. Bring to a boil, then lower the heat slightly and simmer for 60 to 90 minutes, stirring occasionally. Season with salt. We like a soupy consistency, so add a bit more liquid if it thickens too much.

Remove from the heat, season with salt, and ladle into bowls. Top with your desired toppings and serve immediately. Leftover porridge can be cooled and refrigerated for 2 to 4 days. To reheat, stir in additional liquid until it reaches your desired consistency and heat on the stovetop or in the microwave.

THANKSGIVING RICE PORRIDGE

——— GF, DF ———

This rich, meaty version of our *jook* is named for holidays spent in upstate New York at our Aunt Angela and Uncle Wilfried's house. Every year, we'd have a quintessential American Thanksgiving meal—a beautiful turkey, side dishes, all the fixings—and then the turkey carcass would get tossed into a big pot with rice and water to make porridge for breakfast (and lunch and possibly dinner) the next day. Whenever I smell this dish, it brings me back to that holiday feeling of abundance and family. You don't need a big once-a-year turkey either—roast chicken or rib dinner leftovers are great alternatives.

NOTE: It can be a bit of a pain fishing out all the bones, gristle, and other nonedible bits. Possible solutions include wrapping the bones in a neat little package of tied-up cheesecloth, or going Chinese-style and figuring it out as you eat. Regardless, the mouthwatering fragrance of your kitchen will be more than worth it. You can do this with raw meat, like a whole chicken leg, but leftovers with all their glorious browned bits will add much more flavor.

(Continued)

1 cup (185 g) white rice

10 cups (2.4 kg) water or your choice of meat broth or stock

Leftover bones and meat from a roast turkey (or other meat of choice)

Kosher salt

Follow the instructions for Simple Rice Porridge above, adding the bones at the start of cooking. After simmering for at least 90 minutes, let cool slightly. Using tongs, remove the bones and gristle and return any meat back to the pot. Season with salt and serve immediately with toppings of your choice. To reheat, stir in additional liquid until it reaches your desired consistency and heat on the stovetop or in the microwave.

WHOLE GRAIN PORRIDGE

—— V, VV, GF, DF ——

We love the textural and visual variation of mixing another grain with the rice. It's an appealing way to get additional vitamins and nutrients and a seriously satisfying bowl of goodness. Feel free to try other grains, vary the proportions, and experiment with the consistency of your choice.

RICE AND CORNMEAL

¾ cup (150 g) brown rice, or another rice of your choice

¼ cup (45 g) coarse cornmeal or grits

10 cups (2.4 kg) water

Kosher salt

RICE AND QUINOA

¾ cup (150 g) brown rice, or another rice of your choice

¼ cup (45 g) quinoa

10 cups (2.4 kg) water

Kosher salt

Combine the grains and water in a large pot over medium-high heat. Bring to a boil, then lower the heat slightly and simmer for 60 to 90 minutes, stirring occasionally. We like a soupy consistency, so add a splash of liquid if the porridge gets too thick.

Remove from the heat, season with salt, and ladle into bowls. Top with your desired toppings and serve immediately. Leftover porridge can be cooled and refrigerated for 2 to 4 days. To reheat, stir in additional liquid until it reaches your desired consistency and heat on the stovetop or in the microwave.

TOPPINGS

Toppings are really the way to kick this porridge party into gear. Here are a few of our favorites:

PROTEINS

- Seven-minute egg—Our ideal boiled egg with an oozy yolk. Bring water to a boil in a small saucepan and slowly lower 2 to 4 eggs into the water. Simmer for 7 minutes, then transfer to an ice bath to stop the cooking. Peel carefully and slice in half.

- Let's be honest . . . any kind of egg. Try a fried egg or a poached egg—Irene particularly likes stirring in some soft scrambled eggs.

- Red-Cooked Beef (page 158)
- Bacon bits
- Roast Pork Belly (page 166), cut into chunks
- Meat of your choice, cut or shredded into bite-size pieces
- Tofu cubes

SOUR/FERMENTED

- Quick Pickled Carrots (page 24)
- Pickled mustard greens
- Kimchi
- Sauerkraut

SAUCE

- Cranberry Sweet and Sour Sauce (page 15) or Apple Hoisin Sauce (page 16)
- Soy sauce
- Toasted sesame oil
- Sriracha, sambal oelek, or Chili Oil (page 20)
- Ginger Scallion Oil (page 18)

VEGETABLES

- Roasted root vegetables, diced
- Stir-Fried Greens (page 48)
- Charred broccoli or cauliflower
- Sautéed mushrooms
- Sliced or toasted avocado

GARNISH

- Thinly sliced scallions
- Nori
- Herbs such as cilantro, mint, parsley, or basil
- Sesame or hemp seeds
- Fresh or pickled ginger

CRUNCH

- Crushed peanuts
- Fried Shallots (page 21)
- Fried onions
- Fried garlic
- Crushed tortilla chips
- Sliced *youtiao* (aka Chinese crullers)
- Croutons

BEEF AND BROCCOLI

—— GFO, DF ——

In our take on this classic Chinese restaurant dish, both the beef and the broccoli get a lovely char and crunch. We pan-fry a steak to medium-rare and oven-roast the broccoli; if you've only had limp, gloopy takeout versions of this dish, you'll be surprised by the texture and flavor in these florets and stalks. Make sure you peel the broccoli stalk—it gets a bad rap, but the sweet, nutty flavor is fantastic once you get past the tough outer layer.

Serves 4, with rice or other side dishes

BEEF

1 pound (450 g) flank, skirt, or hanger steak

1 tablespoon (15 g) soy sauce (substitute tamari if gluten-free)

1 tablespoon (15 g) Shaoxing wine

2 tablespoons (26 g) neutral oil, such as canola

Kosher salt

BROCCOLI

1½ pounds (675 g) broccoli, stems trimmed, peeled, and cut into chunks, tops cut into florets

¼ cup (52 g) olive oil

½ teaspoon (2 g) kosher salt

SAUCE

1½ teaspoons (6 g) neutral oil, such as canola

2 cloves garlic, minced

One 1-inch piece fresh ginger, minced

3 tablespoons (45 g) oyster sauce

2 tablespoons (40 g) honey

2 tablespoons (30 g) soy sauce (substitute tamari if gluten-free)

1 tablespoon (15 g) water

1 teaspoon (5 g) fish sauce

1 teaspoon (5 g) rice vinegar

GARNISH

¼ cup (20 g) Garlic Panko (page 14; optional, omit if gluten-free)

Zest of 1 lemon (optional)

MARINATE THE BEEF
Combine the beef, soy sauce, wine, and 1 tablespoon of oil in a sealable plastic bag. Marinate for at least 20 minutes while you prepare the broccoli and the sauce, or up to a day in advance.

COOK THE BROCCOLI
Preheat the oven to 425°F (220°C).

Put the broccoli on a baking sheet and drizzle with the oil. Sprinkle with the salt, then use your hands to toss and fully coat the broccoli. Roast for 15 minutes, then carefully flip the pieces of broccoli over with tongs. Roast for another 5 minutes, then check to see if the broccoli has a good char. If not,

continue to roast, checking every 5 minutes, until well browned.

MAKE THE SAUCE
Heat the oil in a medium saucepan over medium-high heat until it shimmers. Add the garlic and ginger and cook until fragrant and softened, about 2 minutes. Add the oyster sauce, honey, soy sauce, water, and fish sauce and bring to a boil. Reduce the heat to medium-low and cook at a low boil for 3 to 5 minutes, stirring occasionally to prevent burning, until thick and sticky. Stir in the vinegar and taste for seasoning; if the sauce is too salty, thin with a little water or meat stock.

COOK THE BEEF

Lay the beef on a cutting board and, if necessary, cut in half crosswise so both pieces fit into your pan. Pat dry with paper towels, then season lightly on both sides with salt. Heat the remaining tablespoon of oil in a large cast-iron or other heavy-bottomed skillet over high heat until lightly smoking. Using tongs, carefully lay the beef pieces flat in the pan and sear until browned on the bottom, about 3 minutes. Flip and brown the other side, about 3 more minutes, turning the heat down if it gets too smoky. This may be enough to cook to our preferred medium rare (125°F/51°C); if you prefer it more well done or have a thick steak, cook for another 3 to 5 minutes. Transfer to a cutting board and let rest for at least 5 minutes before slicing into thin pieces against the grain (across the fibers of the meat).

To serve, put the broccoli and beef on a plate and drizzle with sauce. Sprinkle with panko and lemon zest, if using. Serve immediately with White Rice (page 14) or a side dish of your choice.

MA PO TOFU
WITH APPLE-SCALLION SALAD

—— GFO, DF ——

This classic Sichuan dish features the popular combination of doubanjiang, a fermented bean and chili paste, and Sichuan peppercorns. Together, they bring out *ma la*, or spicy-numbing feeling—a tingly, hot sensation where it feels a bit like your mouth is on fire. If you like it on the spicy end of things, try adding Japones chile like we use at the restaurant, or another chile of your choice. If you prefer a milder dish, leave the chili out altogether—the doubanjiang is enough to add a bit of heat and complexity. The apple-scallion salad acts as a cool compress to soothe all of the numbing spiciness with a fresh hit of crunch and sweetness.

Serves 2 generously or 4 with additional sides like
Stir-Fried Greens (page 48) and White Rice (page 14).

APPLE-SCALLION SALAD

1 sweet-tart apple, such as a Pink Lady, cored and diced or cut into matchsticks

6 scallions, sliced or cut into matchsticks

2 teaspoons (10 g) rice vinegar

2 teaspoons (8 g) toasted sesame oil

MA PO SAUCE

2 tablespoons (26 g) neutral oil, such as canola

1 tablespoon (4 g) Sichuan peppercorns, ground

2 tablespoons (40 g) doubanjiang (substitute with a different chili sauce if gluten-free)

2 cloves garlic, minced

One 1-inch piece fresh ginger, minced

1 dried Japones chile or chile of your choice, chopped or ground, optional

¼ small onion, diced

1 tablespoon (15 g) Shaoxing wine

1 tablespoon (15 g) soy sauce (substitute tamari if gluten-free)

1 tablespoon (10 g) fermented black beans, rinsed and chopped

½ cup (120 g) meat stock or broth

OTHER INGREDIENTS

8 ounces (225 g) ground beef, preferably not too lean

1 pound (450 g) firm or extra-firm tofu, cut into ½-inch cubes

MAKE THE SALAD

Combine all the ingredients in a medium bowl, toss, and let sit while you make the rest of the meal.

MAKE THE SAUCE

Heat the oil in a medium saucepan over medium-low heat until shimmering. Add the peppercorns and lightly toast for 2 minutes. Add the doubanjiang and stir until mixed and fragrant, about 1 to 2 minutes, then add the garlic, ginger, chile, and onion and cook until softened, 3 to 5 minutes. Add the wine and soy sauce and stir to scrape any browned bits from the bottom of the pan. Add the fermented black beans and stock, turn the heat up to medium, bring to a simmer, and simmer for 10 minutes.

Heat a large skillet over medium heat, add the ground beef, and lightly brown it, breaking it into smaller chunks as it cooks, about 3 to 5 minutes. Add the tofu and ma po sauce and stir, making sure to coat everything in a thin layer of the sauce. This isn't

the sauciest version of ma po out there—if you want more sauce, feel free to double the recipe and eat any leftover sauce with noodles, rice dishes, and more. Simmer for 2 to 3 minutes, until the sauce and tofu are heated through.

Serve over White Rice (page 14) and top with a generous helping of the apple-scallion salad so you get a bit of fresh apple in every bite.

DIM SUM TURNIP CAKES
WITH BACON AND MUSHROOMS

—— VO, VVO, GF ——

Our dad always ordered turnip cakes (*lo bak gao*, sometimes known as radish cake) whenever we went out to dim sum. As kids, we would be thrown off by the unexpected flavor. But now I crave that turnip-y flavor, and we're proud to have it on the restaurant menu in our dad's honor. We use daikon radishes because their high water content makes them easy to grate, but you can go with the turnip of your choice. The traditional version contains Chinese sausage and dried shrimp, but we love just about everything with bacon, including our turnip cakes.

SPECIAL EQUIPMENT: Box grater or food processor, steamer setup, loaf pan or other pan that fits into the steamer

Serves 4 as an appetizer or side dish

1 large or 2 medium daikon (about 20 ounces/570 g), grated

5 slices bacon, chopped (optional)

1½ cups (about 4 ounces/120 g) roughly chopped mushrooms of your choice

1 scallion, thinly sliced

¾ cup (100 g) rice flour

¼ cup (30 g) cornstarch

1 teaspoon (3 g) kosher salt, plus more for pan-frying

½ teaspoon (2 g) sugar

Pinch of white pepper

Neutral oil, such as canola, for pan-frying

VEGETARIAN VERSION

½ cup (60 g) diced onion

2 tablespoons (26 g) neutral oil, such as canola or vegetable

Pinch of kosher salt

Put the radish in a medium saucepan and add 1 cup water. Cover and cook over medium heat for about 15 minutes, stirring occasionally, until softened and mostly translucent. Remove from the heat and set aside to cool.

Meanwhile, cook the bacon in a large skillet over medium heat (or cook the onion in the oil and season with salt for the vegetarian version). Once the bacon starts to brown or the onion starts to soften, add the mushrooms and cook until softened, about 3 minutes. Remove from the heat and stir in the scallion.

Whisk the rice flour, cornstarch, salt, sugar, and white pepper in a large bowl. Add the radish to the dry ingredients and mix. Add the bacon or onion mixture and stir to combine, incorporating the bacon fat or oil from the pan for additional flavor.

Lightly oil a loaf pan, add the radish mixture, then flatten the top with a spatula so it cooks evenly. Set up a steamer or stockpot with a steamer rack, add a few inches of water and put the loaf pan inside. Turn the heat to high, cover, and steam for 45 to 60 minutes, or until the cake is firm to the touch. Carefully remove the pan from the pot, let cool for at least 20 minutes, then cut into slices 1-inch thick.

Although the cake is tasty when steamed, we find the crunchy, pan-seared edges to be the best part. To pan-fry, heat a thin layer of neutral oil in a skillet and sear on all sides until browned and crisp. Season with salt and serve with Apple Hoisin Sauce (page 16), Cranberry Sweet and Sour Sauce (page 15), or another sweet and savory sauce of your choice.

CRANBERRY SWEET AND SOUR STIR-FRIED PORK

—— GF, DF ——

You may be surprised to learn a common cooking ingredient in Chinese cooking, and the usual base of sweet and sour sauce: good old ketchup. While we love ketchup, we've gone for a fresher, local take by using cranberries in our sauce. Stir-frying instead of deep-frying also makes this version a bit healthier and easier to execute. Our last innovation (the brainchild of our opening co-chef Max) is serving the pork over a crunchy rice patty, pan-fried like a burger. I find great joy in cracking my fork through a golden brown crust with each bite. You could serve it with plain rice, but we say go GBD (Golden Brown Delicious, thanks Max) or go home. Serve with a side such as Stir-Fried Greens (page 48).

Serves 4, with sides

PORK

1 pound (450 g) pork loin, sliced into ¼-inch-thick strips

2 tablespoons (26 g) neutral oil, such as canola

1 tablespoon (15 g) Shaoxing wine

1 tablespoon (7 g) cornstarch

½ teaspoon (2 g) kosher salt

2 cloves garlic, minced

One ½-inch piece fresh ginger, minced

¼ cup (60 g) Cranberry Sweet and Sour Sauce (page 15), or to taste

2 scallions, thinly sliced, for garnish

RICE CAKES

1 recipe just-cooked White Rice (page 14; do not rinse before cooking)

2 tablespoons (30 g) rice vinegar

2 teaspoons (12 g) miso paste

1 teaspoon (4 g) sugar

½ teaspoon (2 g) kosher salt, or as needed.

Neutral oil, such as canola, for cooking

MAKE THE PORK

Combine the pork, 1 tablespoon of the oil, the wine, cornstarch, and salt in a small bowl. Mix thoroughly and let sit for 15 to 20 minutes.

MAKE THE RICE CAKES

Let the rice cool slightly. Meanwhile, combine the rice vinegar, miso, sugar, and salt in a small bowl and whisk until smooth. Pour the miso-vinegar over the hot rice and stir with a wooden spoon or spatula to combine. Make sure to get under the rice with the spoon to release steam and coat the rice completely.

Taste and add salt or sugar as desired. Using the same spoon, separate the rice in half with a vertical line and then again with a horizontal line, dividing the rice into four equal parts.

Heat a thin film of oil in a large nonstick skillet over medium-high heat until shimmering. At this point, the rice should be sticky and reasonably cool; if not, wait a few more minutes. Wet your hands and grab one quarter of the rice with both hands. Form it into a ball, then flatten it between your palms into a burger-style patty. Place in the pan, then repeat with the remaining rice. Pan-fry for 3 to 5 minutes, until

golden brown, then flip and repeat on the other sides, adding more oil if needed. Transfer to a plate to cool while you cook the pork.

COOK THE PORK

Heat the remaining 1 tablespoon oil in the same skillet over medium heat until shimmering. Add the garlic and ginger and cook for about 2 minutes, until fragrant and lightly softened. Add the pork and fry, stirring occasionally, until cooked through, 3 to 5 minutes. Put into a medium bowl and toss with the cranberry sweet and sour sauce. Taste and add salt or more sauce as desired.

To plate, each person gets a rice cake topped with a scoop of pork and garnished with a flurry of scallions.

DAN DAN NOODLES
WITH CRISPY PORK BELLY AND BRUSSELS SPROUTS

—— DF ——

Welcome to our take on a Sichuan street snack that appears in many different incarnations in both China and the United States. Spiced liberally with fruity Chili Oil and tingly with Sichuan peppercorns, it's a dish known for aggressively zinging your taste buds. At the restaurant, we smooth it out with peanut butter and top it with crunchy, fatty bites of pork belly and stir-fried Brussels sprouts. We like a springy ramen noodle to stand up to the full-bodied sauce, but feel free to substitute the noodle of your choice. Serve with Stir-Fried Greens (page 48), Honey–Soy Butter Glazed Roots (page 108), or something light, like the Beekeeper's Salad (page 96).

Serves 2 with leftovers, 4 with sides

DAN DAN SAUCE

One 2-inch piece fresh ginger, minced

2 cloves garlic, minced

Heaping ½ teaspoon (3 g) Sichuan peppercorns, ground

2 small dried red chilies, minced, or 1 tablespoon (5 g) chili flakes (optional)

⅓ cup (80 g) chicken broth or stock, or water, or more as needed

¼ cup (60 g) unsweetened peanut butter, preferably a natural version with only peanuts

¼ cup (50 g) Chili Oil (page 20) or store-bought chili oil, or more to taste

3 tablespoons (45 g) soy sauce

1 tablespoon (15 g) Apple Hoisin Sauce (page 16) or store-bought hoisin sauce

1 tablespoon (15 g) black vinegar

1 tablespoon (10 g) Chinese sesame paste or tahini

1 teaspoon (7 g) honey

Kosher salt

OTHER INGREDIENTS

Kosher salt

1 pound (450 g) ramen noodles, preferably fresh or frozen, or 12 ounces (340 g) dried noodle of your choice

Neutral oil, for tossing the noodles and cooking (optional)

8 ounces (225 g) Roast Pork Belly (page 166), cut into bite-size chunks, or ground pork

2 cups (165 g) trimmed and thinly sliced Brussels sprouts

¼ cup (30 g) crushed peanuts, for garnish

2 scallions, thinly sliced, for garnish

MAKE THE SAUCE

Combine the ginger, garlic, peppercorns, and chilies in a medium bowl or food processor and mix thoroughly. Add the remaining sauce ingredients and whisk or pulse until the mixture is uniform and relatively smooth. Depending on whether you've used broth or water and the type of peanut butter, you'll want a pinch of salt or more liquid if you prefer a thinner consistency.

MAKE THE NOODLES

Bring a large pot of salted water to boil and cook the noodles according to the package directions until just tender. Drain, toss with a splash of neutral oil, and lay out on a plate so the noodles don't overcook.

COOK THE MEAT

While the noodles are cooking, heat a wok or medium skillet over medium-high heat. If you're using a nonstick skillet or including pork belly with its ample layer of fat, you shouldn't need any oil; otherwise, add a splash of neutral oil to the pan. Add the pork and cook until browned (if using ground pork, make sure it's cooked through). Add the Brussels sprouts, toss with the pork, and cook until the Brussels sprouts are bright green and lightly charred, about 4 minutes.

Transfer the noodles to a large serving bowl and top with the pork and Brussels sprouts. Spoon most of the sauce on top and toss to combine. Taste for seasoning and add more sauce or chili oil if desired. Top with crushed peanuts and sliced scallions and serve immediately.

JJAJANG LAMB NOODLES

—— DF ——

This dark, rich noodle dish is our mishmash take on Chinese *zha jiang mian* (translation: fried sauce noodles) and its Korean counterpart *jjajang myeon*. Like so many Chinese dishes—like so many famous dishes from all cultures—you'll find countless versions, whether it includes sweet bean paste, ground bean paste, black bean paste, or, like ours, just the fermented black beans. It's an earthy Chinese version of the Bolognese we often ate growing up—meaty, thick, and warming. Although the Chinese and Korean versions are typically served with pork, we like how the gaminess of ground lamb stands up to the robust sauce. Serve with sides such as Honey–Soy Butter Glazed Roots (page 108).

Serves 4, with sides

JJAJANG SAUCE

1 tablespoon (13 g) toasted sesame oil

½ medium onion, diced

½ teaspoon (3 g) fish sauce

½ cup (75 g) fermented black beans, rinsed and chopped

3 tablespoons (45 g) Shaoxing wine

2 tablespoons (25 g) sugar

1 tablespoon (15 g) gochujang

⅓ cup (80 g) water

⅓ cup (75 g) silken tofu

NOODLES AND LAMB

Kosher salt

8 ounces (225 g) Chinese wheat noodles, or another noodle with a little chew

1 pound (450 g) ground lamb, preferably not too lean

Neutral oil, such as canola, for cooking (optional)

GARNISH

1 cucumber, julienned or thinly sliced

1 scallion, thinly sliced on the diagonal

¼ medium white onion, diced (optional)

MAKE THE SAUCE

Heat the sesame oil in a medium saucepan over medium-low heat, then add the onion and fish sauce and cook until the onion is softened, about 5 minutes. Add the fermented black beans, wine, sugar, and gochujang and cook for another 2 minutes. Add the water and tofu and cook, stirring to break up any large chunks of tofu, until the sauce thickens and is thoroughly mixed, 3 to 5 minutes. Let cool slightly; puree if desired.

MAKE THE NOODLES AND LAMB

Bring a large pot of salted water to boil for the noodles. Meanwhile, heat a large skillet over medium-high heat. Add the ground lamb and a large pinch of salt and cook, breaking up large pieces with a spatula,

until browned and cooked through, about 7 minutes. Taste for seasoning, then transfer to the pan with the jjajang sauce and stir to combine. Leave the skillet with lamb fat on the stove for stir-frying.

Add the noodles to the water and cook according to the package instructions until just tender. Drain and transfer to the skillet. If there isn't enough fat to lightly coat the bottom, add a splash of neutral oil. Heat over medium heat until the fat or oil shimmers, then add the noodles and stir-fry, letting them lightly brown and get crispy before stirring again. Once the noodles have reached your desired level of crunch, add the lamb and jjajang sauce to the skillet and stir until all the noodles are coated. Transfer to a serving bowl, top with cucumber, scallions, and raw onion, if using, and serve immediately.

STIR-FRIED GREENS

—— V, VV, GFO, DF ——

A simple plate of stir-fried vegetables was often on our childhood table growing up, accompanying anything from roast pork to lasagna. I've come to appreciate this easy, versatile recipe when in need of a quick side dish or something healthy to round out an otherwise indulgent meal. We use whatever local greens our farmers are sending to the restaurant—kale, cabbage, collard greens, turnip greens, beet greens, radicchio, mustard greens and more. At home, it's a nice way to use random leafy greens from the farmers' market or a CSA box, but is also splendid with supermarket greens like curly kale or full-leaf spinach.

If you use something with a thick stem, remove and save in a plastic bag in the fridge or freezer for Traditional-ish Pork Dumplings (page 62), Pierogi Dumplings (page 66), Leafy Greens Gratin (page 110), or elsewhere. Leftovers are fantastic as a topping for Rice Porridge (page 31), mixed into an omelet, or tucked into a sandwich.

Serves 4 as a side dish

1½ tablespoons (20 g) neutral oil, such as canola 2 cloves garlic, thinly sliced	1 bunch (6 to 8 cups) hearty leafy greens, chopped into bite-size pieces Kosher salt	1 tablespoon (13 g) Soy Ginger Dressing (page 14), or 1 teaspoon (5 g) soy sauce (use tamari if gluten-free), 1 teaspoon (4 g) toasted sesame oil, and ½ teaspoon (3 g) rice vinegar	2 tablespoons (10 g) Garlic Panko (page 16; optional, omit if gluten-free)

Heat the oil in a wok or large skillet over medium-high heat until shimmering. Add the garlic and stir until fragrant and lightly browned, about 1 minute. Add the greens, sprinkle lightly with salt, and toss until wilted and well charred in spots. Transfer to a serving bowl and drizzle with the soy ginger dressing. Toss, taste for seasoning and add more sauce if desired. Sprinkle with panko, if desired.

YU XIANG EGGPLANT
WITH CRANBERRIES AND ALMONDS

—— V, GFO, DF ——

This recipe is our take on one of our mom's favorite vegetable dishes, with the unusual addition of dried cranberries and almonds. We like the oomph of the pungent and spicy sauce, made sour by two different vinegars and then rounded out with the subtle sweetness of the cranberries, which seem to melt into the eggplant. What can sometimes be a monochromatic pile of sugary gloop on a plate becomes a punchy yet balanced side dish with contrasting textures; serve over lots of White Rice (page 14) to make it a meal.

Serves 4 as a side dish

YU XIANG SAUCE

1 tablespoon (13 g) neutral oil, such as canola

2 cloves garlic, minced

One 1-inch piece ginger, minced

½ small onion, diced

1 tablespoon (20 g) doubanjiang (substitute another

chili sauce if gluten-free)

¼ cup (60 g) Shaoxing wine

2 tablespoons (30 g) rice vinegar

1 tablespoon (20 g) honey

1 tablespoon (15 g) black vinegar (substitute rice vinegar if gluten-free)

1 teaspoon (5 g) soy sauce (substitute tamari if gluten-free)

2 teaspoons (5 g) cornstarch

1 tablespoon (15 g) water

OTHER INGREDIENTS

Neutral oil, such as canola, for cooking

1 pound (450 g) eggplant (typically 2 Chinese or Japanese eggplants or 1 Italian eggplant), cut into 1-inch chunks

¼ cup (60 g) almonds, whole or sliced

⅓ cup (50 g) dried cranberries

1 scallion, thinly sliced, for garnish

MAKE THE SAUCE

Heat the oil in a medium saucepan over high heat until shimmering. Add the garlic, ginger, onion, and doubanjiang and cook until softened, about 3 minutes. Turn the heat down to medium-low, add the wine, rice vinegar, honey, black vinegar, and soy sauce, and bring to a simmer.

While the sauce heats, whisk the cornstarch with the water in a small bowl to form a slurry. Once the sauce reaches a simmer, turn off the heat and whisk in the slurry to thicken.

COOK THE EGGPLANT

Pour a thin layer of oil into a large skillet and heat over high heat until lightly smoking. Add the eggplant and cook until well browned and softened, 4 to 6 minutes. Remove from the heat and add the eggplant to the sauce. Put the almonds into the pan in which you cooked the eggplant and lightly toast for 2 to 3 minutes. If using whole almonds, crush them (we pop them in a plastic bag and smash them with a rolling pin). Mix half of the almonds into the eggplant along with half of the cranberries, reserving the rest for garnish. Taste for seasoning, then transfer to a serving plate and sprinkle with the remaining cranberries and almonds and the scallions.

CH. 3

DUMPLINGS AND PANCAKES

Dumplings and scallion pancakes have been favorite foods of ours since we learned to make them on our wooden kitchen table as kids. This table represents warmth and family, creation and play. It's still polished and glossy, but scarred from the dings of rolling pins and the vivacious, elbow-bumping action of countless family dinners. We shaped dough into snakes and snails, rolled them into discs, then fried the scallion-studded pancakes to hot, savory, straight-out-the-pan-burn-your-tongue perfection. These food memories are dear to us and sparked a lifelong connection to these Chinese snacks. But even if you didn't grow up rolling dough by hand, it's hard to deny the allure of plump, crispy-bottomed dumplings stuffed with juicy pork or spiced veggies. I have yet to meet anyone who can turn down a golden brown wedge of pancake layered with fragrant scallions and waiting to be doused in a garlicky soy dipping sauce.

Making Scallion Pancakes (page 74) from scratch, with their meditative kneading process and the joy of watching dough slowly take shape under your hands, is ideal for the right moments. But we also find that pulling a premade scallion pancake straight from the freezer, peeling off its plastic casing, and placing it directly into hot oil is its own joyful act, one that I had perfected by high school for almost daily afternoon snacks. We brought this childhood love to the food truck menu and transformed it into a modern street snack, stuffing scallion pancakes with braised beef and griddled potatoes, Vermont Brie and roasted parsnips, and Chinese spiced pulled pork and cheddar. These scallion pancake sandwiches won rave reviews, but it wasn't until we started playing around with our own staff meals that we stumbled upon our award-winning signature dish. The Double Awesome (page 77) can now be yours at home, whether you roll out a pancake by hand or pick one up at your local market. And once you've embraced scallion pancakes as bread, you can make Irene's favorite Kimchi Dog (page 80) or stuff with any sandwich filling you like. The possibilities are endless—have fun with it!

We also encourage you to go wild when it comes to dumpling fillings. You'll probably notice that we don't follow anyone's notion of culinary authenticity, with recipes ranging from Beef and Blue Cheese Dumplings (page 64) to Pierogi Dumplings (page 66). We do have a version of a traditional Pork Dumpling—well, traditional-ish—on page 62, but even that we encourage you to tweak based on what you've got in your kitchen. Invite your vegan friends over to help you make Three Sisters Dumplings (page 69), or use a recipe as a starting point for your ideal ingredients. Growing up, our parents loved having friends over for dumpling folding parties. It's a great activity for people of all ages: dinner party, entertainment, and a learning experience all rolled up into one. Make the dough in advance so it has time to rest, or pick up some premade wrappers. Prepare a few bowls of filling, set up some folding stations, and set out a sauce bar so everyone can create, experiment, and share in the dumpling party fun.

Soon enough, your kitchen table might be a bit banged up by rolling pins, but each scuff represents a memory of friends crowded around your table, practicing their folding techniques and jostling for the nearest dipping sauce. Your kitchen might end up covered in flour, but we bet people will leave with smiles on their faces. Now that's a tradition we can get behind.

DOUBLE AWESOME CHINESE FOOD

HOT WATER DOUGH

—— V, VV, DF ——

We use this basic dough for our childhood favorites of scallion pancakes and dumplings. It's a fun and forgiving dough for kids to work with, although parental sous chefs should probably be in charge of the hot water steps.

Makes enough dough for one dumpling recipe
(about 24 dumplings)
or one Scallion Pancake recipe (page 74)

2 cups (240 g)
all-purpose flour

¼ teaspoon (1 g)
kosher salt

1 cup (240 g) water,
boiled and let cool for
about 1 minute

Mix the flour and salt in a large bowl. Using a wooden spoon, slowly stir in ¾ cup (180 g) of the hot water until a ball is formed and all the flour is incorporated. If the flour in the bottom of the bowl is not sticking to the ball, slowly drizzle in more water 1 teaspoon at a time and continue to stir.

When all the flour has come together into a ball and the dough is cool enough to handle, place on a lightly floured surface and knead until smooth and elastic, 3 to 5 minutes. If necessary, add a sprinkle of flour to keep the dough from sticking to your hands or work surface. Place back in the bowl, cover with a damp cloth, and leave to rest for 30 to 60 minutes so the gluten can relax and the dough is easier to shape. When making in advance, the dough can rest in the fridge a day or two wrapped in lightly oiled plastic wrap. Bring to room temperature before using.

DUMPLING MAKING

Each of the recipes in this chapter makes about 24 dumplings, depending on the size of your wrappers and how you fold them. If the filling includes raw meat, fry or microwave a tablespoon of filling to test for seasoning before you start folding. It'll make dinner for four people with sides, or for one or two with lots of leftovers. All the recipes can easily be doubled, tripled, or more, so you have some to eat, some to freeze, and some to send home with your friends. We firmly believe in spreading the dumpling love.

MAKE THE DUMPLING WRAPPERS

Using a sharp knife or dough cutter, slice the ball of Hot Water Dough into four equal pieces. Set one aside on a cutting board and cover the remaining pieces with a damp towel so they don't dry out. Roll the dough ball with your hands to form a roughly 6-inch-long "snake" (see photos for a visual guide). Cut the snake into six equal pieces. Turn each piece onto its side and flatten with your hand slightly, then use a dowel or rolling pin to flatten into circles 2 to 3 millimeters thick and about 3 inches in diameter.

FOLD THE DUMPLINGS

When we teach dumpling classes at our restaurant, we demonstrate the classic pleated, crescent-shaped style along with the pyramid (see page 72) and the folded empanada (which turns into the tortellini), but we encourage you to play around!

For the classic pleat (see page 68), hold a wrapper in your left hand and place a spoonful of filling into the center with your right hand. Depending on how large you've rolled your wrappers, this is usually about ¾ tablespoon to 1 tablespoon. Leave some space: tempting as it is to overstuff, the filling will squirt messily and make the folding process more difficult.

Fold the wrapper in half into a taco shape and, starting from the right side, pinch the wrapper shut. (If you're using store-bought wrappers, set up a small bowl of water to help seal the wrappers. Dip a finger into the water and smear it around the edge of each wrapper before you fold so the dough sticks when you

pinch it shut.) After each pinch, fold the side farthest from you into a pleat toward the pinched end and press it back together. The side closest to you should remain smooth and will gradually curve toward you into a crescent shape.

Continue to pleat and pinch until the entire dumpling is sealed, aiming for 5 or 6 pleats per dumpling or more if you want to get fancy. As you fold, place the dumplings onto a large plate or baking sheet in rows with a little space between each one. Cook them right away, or place the sheet into the freezer so they can freeze without squishing each other. Once frozen, transfer the dumplings into plastic bags for storage.

COOK THE DUMPLINGS

At home, we always use a pan-searing/steaming technique, which results in a nice crispy sear on the bottom of the dumpling and a chewy steamed top. This technique works with raw or frozen dumplings and only uses one pan. Fewer dishes = more time to eat dumplings.

Find a large skillet (nonstick works well here) for which you have a lid. Coat the bottom of the skillet with a layer of neutral oil (about 2 tablespoons) and heat over medium-high heat. Once the oil is hot and shimmery, carefully fill the pan with a single layer of dumplings (non-pleated side down), leaving a bit of room between each one. Cook for 2 to 4 minutes, until the bottoms are golden brown—you can pick one up to check.

Turn the heat to medium and grab the lid and

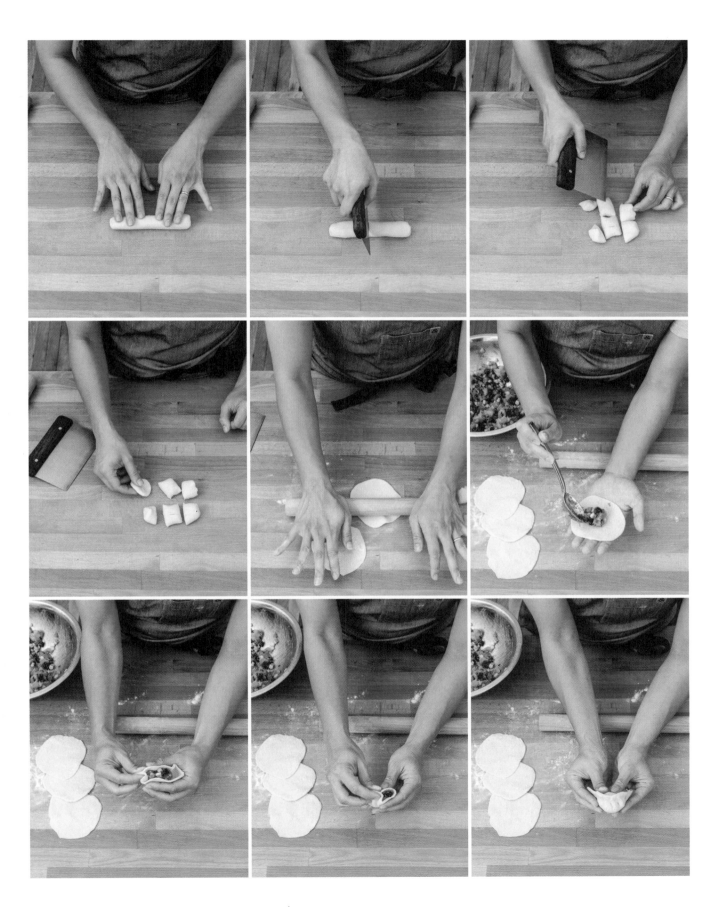

about ¼ cup water. Shielding yourself with the lid, pour the water into the hot pan—it will steam and sizzle, so be careful there isn't too much oil in the pan to spatter all over the place. Cover the pan and let the steam cook the top of the dumplings, 4 to 6 minutes, or 8 to 10 minutes if cooking from frozen.

Once the water has evaporated, the wrappers should be slightly translucent and the filling fully cooked. If not, add a splash of water and cover again for a minute or two. You can test for doneness by breaking open a dumpling or using your instant-read thermometer. Turn the heat up slightly, and the remaining oil in the bottom of the pan will re-crisp the bottom of the dumplings. Depending on your heat, water, and oil levels, you may need to add more water or oil, but you'll get the hang of it after practice, we promise.

A FEW NOTES: Traditionally, pan-seared dumplings are only fried on the bottom, but I often flip the dumplings over for an additional sear. It adds more crunch and flavor and can help if you're using premade wrappers, which sometimes are dry around the edges. We deep-fry many of our dumplings at the restaurant for a crackly, golden exterior. For a healthier and easy-to-cook alternative, our mom loves dumplings steamed or boiled in water or broth. As cultures all around the world have learned, food wrapped in dough is fantastic cooked in a multitude of ways. Have fun with it and experiment with your own fillings, folds, and cooking techniques. As the saying (that we definitely made up) goes: the world is your dumpling.

Helpful steps and equipment for dumpling feasts:

- If you're making your own dough, set out multiple sets of rolling pins and cutting boards.

- If you're using premade wrappers (we like Twin Marquis brand), set out small shallow bowls of water and wet paper towels to keep the wrappers moist.

- Prepare large bowls of dumpling fillings—consider a selection of meat, vegetarian, and vegan options, depending on your guests.

- Set up a sauce bar with small bowls for everyone to make their own dipping sauce—we like to include soy sauce, black vinegar, an infused oil, hot sauce, and a homemade aioli (page 23).

- Set up a skillet for pan-searing and/or a steamer setup or pot of boiling water for steaming or boiling dumplings. We typically cook about half the dumplings and freeze the remaining.

- Make sure you have flat trays that fit in your freezer for all the uncooked dumplings—line up raw dumplings on top with a bit of space in between each one. Once frozen, place into labeled plastic bags for your guests to take home.

TRADITIONAL-ISH PORK DUMPLINGS

—— DF ——

This is our take on the traditional Chinese pork dumpling, made with thoroughly untraditional vegetable scraps. Most recipes call for napa cabbage or Chinese chives, which are wonderful but not often found in your average kitchen. Save the stems from Stir-Fried Greens (page 48) or Magical Kale Salad (page 95) or hoard carrot tops or beet greens—the vegetable options abound.

Makes about 24 dumplings

1 cup diced tightly packed green vegetable of your choice, such as Brussels sprouts, kale stems, or turnip greens

One 1-inch piece fresh ginger, minced

5 cloves garlic, minced

2 tablespoons (30 g) soy sauce

2 tablespoons (26 g) toasted sesame oil

1 large egg

¾ teaspoon (2 g) kosher salt

8 ounces (225 g) ground pork, preferably not too lean

1 recipe Hot Water Dough (page 57) or 24 store-bought dumpling wrappers

Neutral oil, such as canola, for cooking

Soy Vinegar Dipping Sauce (page 15) or Sriracha Aioli (page 23), for serving

Put all the filling ingredients except the pork in a large bowl and stir to combine. Add the pork and mix thoroughly. Pan-fry or microwave a spoonful to taste for seasoning and adjust as needed. Follow the instructions for rolling and cooking dumplings (pages 58 to 61) and serve with dipping sauce or aioli.

BEEF AND BLUE CHEESE DUMPLINGS

With top billing on our very first food truck menu, these dumplings flaunt our passion for combining Chinese food and cheese. We experimented with all kinds of beef and cheese combinations (try Red-Cooked Beef Stew, page 158, with sharp cheddar) but have a particular allegiance to this one, with its unexpected funky hit of blue cheese.

Makes about 24 dumplings

10 ounces (285 g) ground beef

½ cup (75 g) crumbled blue cheese

1 large egg

1 tablespoon (15 g) Apple Hoisin Sauce (page 16) or store-bought hoisin sauce, plus more for serving (optional)

1 tablespoon (5 g) panko, or other breadcrumbs

2 teaspoons (10 g) soy sauce

1 teaspoon (5 g) fish sauce

Pinch of white pepper

1 recipe Hot Water Dough (page 57) or 24 store-bought dumpling wrappers

Neutral oil, such as canola, for cooking

Soy Vinegar Dipping Sauce (page 15), for serving

Place all the ingredients for the filling in a large bowl and mix thoroughly. Pan-fry or microwave a spoonful to taste for seasoning and adjust as necessary. Follow the instructions for rolling and cooking dumplings (pages 58 to 61), making sure each dumpling gets some blue cheese. Serve with hoisin sauce or soy vinegar dipping sauce.

SWEET POTATO, FETA, AND BROWN BUTTER DUMPLINGS

—— V ——

Casting about for compelling vegetarian dumpling ideas in the early days of the food truck, the stalwart of many wedding catering menus came to mind: butternut squash and brown butter ravioli. We've breathed some new life into the dish with briny chunks of feta, the earthy heft of sweet potatoes, and, of course, the always-beloved magic of crispy dumpling skin.

Makes about 24 dumplings

1 pound (450 g) sweet potatoes (about 2 medium-large potatoes)

4 tablespoons (2 ounces/55 g) unsalted butter

½ small onion, diced

1 clove garlic, minced

5 fresh sage leaves, minced

½ cup (75 g) crumbled feta cheese

¼ teaspoon (1 g) kosher salt

1 recipe Hot Water Dough (page 57) or 24 store-bought dumpling wrappers

Neutral oil, such as canola, for cooking

Soy Aioli (page 23) or Soy Vinegar Dipping Sauce (page 15), for serving

Preheat the oven to 425°F (220°C).

Wrap the sweet potatoes in aluminum foil and place on a baking sheet or baking dish. Roast for 45 minutes, or until they can easily be pierced by a fork.

Meanwhile, place the butter in a small saucepan and turn the heat to medium. Let the butter cook, stirring occasionally, until the milk solids start to brown and it smells nutty, about 8 minutes. Add the onion and garlic and cook for 2 minutes, turning the heat down to low if the butter starts to darken more than a medium brown. Add the sage and cook for another 2 minutes, then remove from the heat and set aside to cool.

Unwrap the sweet potatoes and let them cool, then remove and discard the skins. Place the sweet potatoes in a large bowl and add the brown butter–sage mixture, the cheese, and salt. Mash everything together until the mixture is thoroughly combined, leaving a few sweet potato chunks for texture. Follow the instructions for rolling and cooking dumplings (pages 58 to 61) and serve with soy aioli or soy vinegar dipping sauce.

PIEROGI DUMPLINGS

—— v ——

Abounding in local potatoes during a New England winter, we dreamed of Eastern European pierogi dancing alongside Chinese *jiao zi*. Like mashed potatoes in a post-Thanksgiving sandwich or any of our kitchen manager Peter's cherished starch-on-starch snacks, the potato-wrapped-in-dough idea is as cozy and satisfying as a warm blanket, especially in combination with sharp cheddar cheese. Don't peel the potatoes, just rinse off any dirt. Not only do we want to save you the effort, mess and waste, but the peels add texture and contrast alongside the veggie bits of your choice.

Makes about 24 dumplings

1 pound (450 g) potatoes, such as russet, cut into 1-inch pieces	2 cloves garlic, minced	¼ teaspoon (1 g) kosher salt	Neutral oil, such as canola, for cooking
4 tablespoons (2 ounces/55 g) unsalted butter	½ to 1 cup diced vegetables, such as broccoli, carrots, or kale stems (use less if stems, more if leafy)	Freshly ground black pepper	Applesauce and sour cream, or Soy Aioli (page 23), for serving
1 small onion, diced	½ cup (60 g) grated sharp cheddar cheese	1 recipe Hot Water Dough (page 57) or 24 store-bought dumpling wrappers	

Put the potatoes in a medium pot, cover with cold water, and bring to a boil over high heat. Reduce the heat and simmer until the largest piece can easily be pierced by a fork, 10 to 12 minutes. Drain and return the potatoes to the empty pot, place back on the still-warm stove, and let the potatoes release steam for a few minutes to reduce the amount of moisture in the filling.

Meanwhile, melt 2 tablespoons of the butter in a medium saucepan over medium-low heat. Add the onion and garlic and cook until softened but not colored. Add the diced vegetables and cook until wilted or softened, 2 to 4 minutes, then remove the pan from the heat.

Combine the potatoes with the remaining 2 tablespoons butter, the cheese, salt, a few turns of pepper, and the vegetable mixture in the pot (or transfer to a large bowl). Mash gently with a large fork or potato masher until the potatoes are mostly broken down with some small chunks for texture. Taste for seasoning; it should be scrumptious enough to pile into a bowl and eat with a spoon.

Let cool, then follow the instructions for rolling and cooking dumplings (pages 58 to 61). Serve with spoonfuls of applesauce and sour cream, like we do at Mei Mei, or soy aioli for dipping.

CRANBERRY SAGE PORK DUMPLINGS

—— DF ——

We love the New England ingredient meets Chinese technique at Thanksgiving dinner vibe of these dumplings. Hat tip to our friends Heather and Brad at The Piggery for the cranberry sage sausage idea, and for being all-around badass farmers and pig people.

Makes about 24 dumplings

1 tablespoon (13 g) neutral oil, such as canola

5 fresh sage leaves, minced

2 cloves garlic, minced

¼ medium onion, minced

⅓ cup (50 g) dried cranberries, chopped

12 ounces (340 g) ground pork, preferably not too lean

1½ teaspoons (5 g) kosher salt

1 recipe Hot Water Dough (page 57) or 24 store-bought dumpling wrappers

Neutral oil, such as canola, for cooking

Soy Vinegar Dipping Sauce (page 15) or Cranberry Sweet and Sour Sauce (page 15), for serving

Heat the oil in a small skillet over medium heat until shimmering. Add the sage, garlic, and onion and cook until softened, about 4 minutes. Set aside to cool.

Mix the cranberries and pork in a medium bowl. Add the cooled sage and onion mixture and salt and stir to combine. Cook 1 tablespoon to test for seasoning, then follow the instructions for rolling and cooking dumplings (pages 58 to 61). Serve with soy vinegar dipping sauce or cranberry sweet and sour sauce.

THREE SISTERS DUMPLINGS

—— V, VV ——

These dumplings are named for the indigenous agricultural tradition of growing corn, beans, and squash together, primarily known from the Haudenosaunee (Iroquois) nations. The plants thrive in this symbiotic relationship, also known as interplanting—the corn provides a stalk for the beans, the beans fix nitrogen to help fertilize the soil, and the squash shades the ground, reducing weed growth and preserving moisture. These dumplings nod to indigenous agriculture and the indigenous peoples of the Northeast region and underscore the importance of farming that is holistic and supports a healthy soil and ecosystem.

NOTE: We make this with a whole butternut squash. Once a cup has been set aside for the dumplings (usually about one-quarter of a 2-pound/900-g squash), cut the remaining squash into chunks for the Wheat Berry Salad (page 140) or the Farmers' Market Fried Rice (page 119). If using precut chunks, the recipe requires about ½ pound squash; toss in olive oil and lightly sprinkle with salt before roasting for 25 to 30 minutes.

Makes about 24 dumplings

BUTTERNUT SQUASH MASH

1 butternut squash (about 2 pounds/ 900 g)

1 tablespoon (13 g) extra-virgin olive oil

½ teaspoon (2 g) kosher salt

¼ cup (60 g) water

OTHER INGREDIENTS

¾ cup (130 g) cooked black beans; if canned, drained and rinsed

¾ cup (120 g) corn kernels, fresh or frozen and thawed

Leaves from 2 to 3 thyme sprigs

2 cloves garlic, minced

2 tablespoons (26 g) extra-virgin olive oil

¼ teaspoon (1 g) kosher salt

1 recipe Hot Water Dough (page 57) or 24 store-bought dumpling wrappers

Neutral oil, such as canola, for cooking

Soy Aioli (page 23) or Soy Vinegar Dipping Sauce (page 15), for serving

MAKE THE SQUASH

Preheat the oven to 450°F (230°C).

Using a sharp knife, carefully cut the top and bottom off the squash, then stand it upright and slice it lengthwise down the middle. Scoop out and discard the seeds, then place the two halves cut-side up in a baking dish. Drizzle with the oil and sprinkle with the salt. Pour the water into the base of the pan, cover with aluminum foil, and bake for 45 minutes, or until you can easily slide a fork into the largest part of the squash. Cool, then scoop out 1 cup (200 g) of the flesh and reserve the rest for other uses. Stored in an airtight container, it will keep in the fridge for 3 to 5 days.

MAKE THE FILLING

Combine the beans, corn, thyme, and garlic in a medium bowl. Add the reserved 1 cup squash, the oil, and salt and mix thoroughly. Taste for seasoning, then follow the instructions for rolling and cooking dumplings (pages 58 to 61).

Serve with the soy aioli or the soy vinegar dipping sauce as a vegan option.

CHORIZO DUMPLINGS
WITH WHITE BEAN PUREE AND CILANTRO OIL

——— DF ———

Boston Magazine said this dumpling "might just be the best two-bite morsel in town" in their award write-up for best dumplings in the city. To be honest, the credit should really go to Brad and Heather at The Piggery for their traditionally raised heritage breed pigs that they turn into some damn good chorizo. Hence this recipe is really about sourcing the best chorizo you can find. We will take credit for pairing it with this white bean puree, which serves as a creamy (but vegan!) foil to the piquancy of the chorizo spices—but begs to be eaten on its own as a dip, a sandwich spread, or straight from the bowl with a spoon.

Makes about 24 dumplings

DUMPLINGS

13½ ounces (380 g) raw (not cured) chorizo sausage, casing removed if necessary

1 recipe Hot Water Dough (page 57) or 24 store-bought dumpling wrappers

WHITE BEAN PUREE

One 15-ounce can white beans, such as cannellini, drained and rinsed (265 g, or about 1½ cups cooked beans)

⅔ cup (160 g) water

2 cloves garlic, sliced

¼ small onion, minced

½ cup (105 g) extra-virgin olive oil

½ teaspoon (2 g) kosher salt

Pinch of ground white pepper

CILANTRO OIL

1 bunch cilantro, roughly chopped

1 cup (210 g) neutral oil, such as canola

Roll the chorizo into dumplings and cook, following the instructions on page 58.

MAKE THE WHITE BEAN PUREE

Place the beans, water, garlic, and onion in a small saucepan over medium heat. Cover and cook for 10 minutes. Remove from the heat and let cool.

Transfer the bean mixture to a blender and add the oil, salt, and white pepper. Blend until smooth, thinning with an additional splash of water, if desired. Taste for seasoning.

MAKE THE CILANTRO OIL

Combine the cilantro and oil and mash in a mortar and pestle or blend in a blender. Strain through cheesecloth, if desired.

To serve, smear a heaping spoonful of the white bean puree onto a plate and place a few dumplings on top. Drizzle with cilantro oil.

CUMIN LAMB DUMPLINGS
WITH MINT YOGURT

We love how this dish showcases local lamb with some of its best friends across global cuisines. We season the lamb briskly with cumin, a nod to the northwestern Chinese region of Xinjiang and the lamb and cumin stir-fries of the Uyghur people. Adding to the sensory experience are the aromatic tingles of Sichuan peppercorn and fiery breath of chili that together characterize Sichuan cooking. We veer away from China with a cooling sauce that salutes the traditional English pairing of lamb with mint while celebrating the Mediterranean love affair of lamb and yogurt.

Makes about 24 dumplings

MINT YOGURT

½ cup (about 12 sprigs) fresh mint leaves, finely chopped

1 cup (227 g) plain whole Greek yogurt, or strained yogurt

1 clove garlic, finely minced or grated

Kosher salt

LAMB FILLING

1 heaping teaspoon (2 g) Sichuan peppercorns

2 teaspoons (5 g) cumin seeds

1 small dried red chile or 1 teaspoon chili flakes (2 g), or more if desired

10 ounces (285 g) ground lamb

¼ small onion, diced

1 teaspoon (5 g) fish sauce

1½ tablespoons (22 g) soy sauce

Kosher salt

OTHER INGREDIENTS

1 recipe Hot Water Dough (page 57) or 24 store-bought dumpling wrappers

Neutral oil, such as canola, for cooking

MAKE THE MINT YOGURT

Combine all the ingredients a small bowl and add a good pinch of salt. Taste for seasoning and adjust as needed, then let sit for at least 15 minutes or up to overnight in the refrigerator before serving.

MAKE THE DUMPLINGS

Combine the Sichuan peppercorns, cumin seeds, and chile in a small skillet over medium heat. Toast until fragrant, about 2 minutes, shaking the pan occasionally. Let cool, then grind in a mortar and pestle or spice grinder.

Combine the lamb, onion, fish sauce, and soy sauce in a large bowl, add the ground spices, and mix thoroughly. Fry a small piece in a pan to check for seasoning; you may not need additional salt as the fish sauce and soy sauce will help season the mixture. Follow the instructions for rolling and cooking dumplings (pages 58 to 61). Serve with the mint yogurt for dipping.

SCALLION PANCAKES

—— V, VV, DF ——

If you've ever had these flaky fried discs dotted with slivers of green onions, you know they can be seriously addictive. When you have perfected the quick and easy scallion pancake recipe to the point that it only takes you an hour or less to make, it's dangerous business. We give you this scallion pancake recipe with a warning: with great power comes great responsibility. After trying these pancakes, the mere sizzle of the pan or scent of freshly chopped scallions may cause you to relinquish control, churning out pancake after pancake and consuming every bite. Cook at your own risk . . .

Makes 4 pancakes

1 recipe Hot Water Dough (page 57), rested	¼ cup (52 g) toasted sesame oil	Neutral oil, such as canola, for cooking	Soy Vinegar Dipping Sauce (page 15), for serving
	1⅓ cups (80 g) thinly sliced scallions	Kosher salt	

MAKE THE PANCAKES

Cut the dough into 4 equal pieces. Take one piece and cover the rest with a damp cloth. Roll the piece into a ball, flatten it slightly, then use a rolling pin to flatten it into a circle about 8 inches in diameter. Use a brush (or your fingers) to cover the dough circle with 1 tablespoon of the sesame oil, then sprinkle with ⅓ cup of the scallions.

Roll up the circle into a snake (see photos on page 75 for a visual guide), then twist the snake into a snail-like spiral and tuck the end underneath. Flatten slightly with your hand, then use the rolling pin to roll out again into an 8-inch circle. Stop here, or, if you want more flaky layers, repeat the snake and snail steps and roll out again. Be gentle, as scallions may burst out of the dough as you continue. Repeat with the remaining dough to make 4 pancakes.

COOK THE PANCAKES

Heat a thin layer of neutral oil in a large skillet over medium-high heat until shimmering. Don't skimp on the oil; ample oil is part of the charm of this dish. Carefully slide the pancake into the pan and fry on each side until golden brown, about 3 minutes per side. Sprinkle lightly with salt and place on a paper towel to cool. Repeat with the remaining pancakes. Cut into wedges and serve with soy vinegar dipping sauce. Try not to burn your tongue.

THE DOUBLE AWESOME

—— v ——

This sandwich was made on a whim, but has become beloved in our hometown of Boston. The Double Awesome was invented after we started sous vide-ing eggs en masse and experimenting with staff meals like deep-fried scallion pancake burritos stuffed with runny yolk explosions. One morning, as I was making myself a hurried breakfast, I broke two perfectly cooked eggs onto the grill, found some local greens pesto and Vermont cheddar in the fridge, and tucked it all inside a scallion pancake. On impulse, I added it to the menu, on a day the food truck was parked outside the Boston Public Library. I thought, *Oh man, these eggs are awesome. And two eggs . . . well, that's double awesome*. And thus a sandwich was born.

NOTE: If you've never had a Double Awesome at Mei Mei, you should know that the egg ooziness is vital to glorious enjoyment of the sandwich. Since we don't sous vide at home, we fry the eggs instead. Don't turn your heat up too high and don't smash the egg with your spatula—aim for cooked whites but a lovely gooey, messy yolk. Also essential to the enjoyment of this sandwich are napkins. Lots of 'em.

Serves 2 hungry people

2 tablespoons (26 g) neutral oil, such as canola or vegetable	2 uncooked scallion pancakes (page 74) (or use store-bought) 4 large eggs	⅔ cup (80 g) shredded cheddar cheese (the sharper the better)	2 tablespoons (30 g) Local Greens Pesto (recipe follows) or store-bought pesto

Preheat the oven to 250°F (120°C).

Heat 1 tablespoon of the oil in a skillet large enough to comfortably fit a scallion pancake (ideally nonstick or cast-iron) over medium heat. Once the oil is shimmering, carefully place the pancake into the pan and cook until golden brown on the bottom, about 3 minutes.

Using tongs, flip the pancake over to brown on the other side. Sprinkle ⅓ cup (40 g) of the cheese onto the pancake to melt while the bottom cooks. Once cooked on both sides, use tongs or a spatula to carefully place the pancake, cheese-side up, onto a heatproof plate or tray and place in the oven to stay warm while you cook the second pancake.

Once both pancakes are in the oven, crack the eggs into the pan and lightly fry them, adding more oil if necessary to prevent sticking. To achieve a similar effect to the famous Mei Mei slow-poached-then-fried oozy egg scenario, fry the egg lightly on one side, then flip to lightly brown the other side. The eggs should be cooked and a bit crispy on the outside, and the yolk should still be runny.

Remove a pancake from the oven and place it on a cutting board, cheese-side up. Smear 1 tablespoon of the pesto on half the pancake, then place the two eggs on the pesto side. Use a spatula to fold the pancake in half, covering both eggs, and cut between the eggs to form two pieces of awesome. Repeat with the second pancake.

(Continued)

DOUBLE AWESOME CHINESE FOOD

LOCAL GREENS PESTO

This isn't a classic pesto—no nuts, no cheese—but it's made from the same process that gives pesto its name (from the Italian verb *pestare*, meaning to pound or crush). It's both convenient for people with allergies and easier and cheaper to make at home. Use whatever seasonal greens you get from the market or have at home, including greens that are slightly too wilted or yellowed for a salad. Feel free to make extra; large amounts can be frozen for later use.

Makes 1 cup

4 cups (70 g) greens or herbs of your choice, such as kale, collards, arugula, mustard greens, or basil

⅓ cup (70 g) neutral oil, such as vegetable or canola, plus more if needed

2 tablespoons (30 g) rice vinegar, plus more if needed

3 cloves garlic

Kosher salt

Combine the greens, oil, vinegar, and garlic in a blender and blend until you have an easily spreadable paste. Depending on how tightly packed your greens are, you may need to drizzle in additional oil or vinegar. Season with salt and use immediately or store in an airtight container in the refrigerator for up to a week.

THE KIMCHI DOG

Endless experimentation in the early days of the food truck opened our eyes to the possibilities of scallion pancake as delivery vehicle for exciting fillings. The easiest version goes: 1) fold in half; 2) stuff with stuff. But Irene's Kimchi Dog, where the scallion pancake encircles the hot dog like a warm flaky hug, just might be our favorite. This is really more of an assembly list than an actual recipe, but we hope it inspires you to experiment with all sorts of scallion pancake sandwich ideas of your own.

Serves 1 hungry person

1 tablespoon (13 g) neutral oil, such as vegetable or canola

1 uncooked Scallion Pancake (page 74) (or use store-bought)

1 tablespoon (15 g) Sriracha Aioli (page 23) or 1½ teaspoons (8 g) sriracha mixed with 1½ teaspoons (8 g) mayonnaise

⅓ cup (75 g) kimchi

1 hot dog, cooked

⅓ cup or small handful arugula or greens of your choice

Line a plate with paper towels.

Heat the oil in a skillet large enough to comfortably fit a scallion pancake (ideally nonstick or cast-iron) over medium heat. Once the oil is shimmering, carefully place the pancake into the pan and cook until golden brown on the bottom, 2 to 3 minutes. Using tongs, flip the pancake over to brown on the other side. Place on the prepared plate to cool.

Spread the sriracha aioli in a thick line down the center of the pancake and follow with the kimchi. Place the hot dog on top. If the hot dog is much shorter than the pancake, cut it in half lengthwise and spread out the pieces to ensure hot dog in every bite. Sprinkle with greens and roll up like a burrito, leaving the ends open. Eat immediately.

A few other ideas for scallion pancake sandwiches, rolled or folded:

Ham and Cheese, but Chinese: Sliced deli ham and melted cheddar or Havarti, with a smear of Apple Hoisin Sauce (page 16).

Turkey and Kimchi: Sliced smoked turkey, a scoop of kimchi, some salad greens, and a tablespoon or so of Sriracha Aioli or Soy Aioli (page 23).

Cranberry Pulled Pork: Leftover pork from Five-Spice Pork Shoulder (page 172), a handful of fresh greens or leftover Stir-Fried Greens (page 48), and a spoonful of Cranberry Sweet and Sour Sauce (page 15).

VEGETABLES THROUGH THE SEASONS

Back in early 2012, as we waited for our food truck to be built, we spent our free days volunteering at The Food Project, a community organization with a small urban farm in Boston. We harvested dirt-streaked turnips and magenta stems of rainbow chard. We shoveled compost, trundled wheelbarrows, and scrubbed vegetables. We did whatever was necessary to help this small acre-and-a-half plot in its mission to increase community access to fresh food. Irene had spent time on farms before, but my experience in gardening and farming essentially consisted of raking backyard leaves and trying not to kill houseplants too quickly. Standing knee-deep in piles of decomposing vegetables, trimming sprawling bunches of Red Russian kale, these long but rewarding days at The Food Project reminded us of the effort required to grow and harvest the food we eat and the importance of valuing and appreciating the work of farmers. We felt invigorated to pursue our grand experiment: How could we support small growers while celebrating the bounty of New England vegetables?

Once the truck opened for business, we would drive to nearby farms and buy any available vegetables, praying we'd get enough product to avoid a trip to the restaurant supply warehouse. Essentially a supermarket on steroids, with pallets of processed food reaching two or three stories high, these big-box stores encapsulate the industrialized food system that we're hoping to move away from. They're a far cry from weeding alongside Jess the farm manager and unearthing baby carrots to haul home in a battered orange plastic crate. Now we don't have the time to pick veggies anymore (or, let's be honest, the desire to shovel more compost), but we still believe it's important to support farms like The Food Project as well as larger distributors and suppliers working toward a more just, ethical food system. We buy some ingredients directly from farms in Greater Boston—our friends from Allandale Farm and the Urban Farming Institute often tromp down the restaurant stairs in dusty boots, arms straining from their load of summer squash or rutabaga, then head upstairs for freshly cooked dumplings before driving back to the farm. But we're also constantly researching ways to buy local vegetables that make life easier for us as well as the farmers.

Our larger produce suppliers now include Metro Pedal Power, a farm share bike delivery service that cycles over veggies grown in Greater Boston, as well as two regional farm aggregators and distributors, Farm Fresh and Hudson Valley Harvest. Their websites keep us informed of the latest seasonal offerings from local farmers, so we can snag the first parsnips to come out of the ground for Spring Dug Parsnip Soup (page 88) or the last of the beets in storage for Hot and Sour Borscht (page 91). We know when there's a glut of kale for Magical Kale Salad (page 95) or when someone's looking to unload five cases of cucumbers at a great price so we can run a Smacked Cucumber Salad (page 92) special. It's the modern, tech-savvy, restaurant-friendly version of the farmers' market, which we still try to visit in our free time.

While you're probably not in need of five cases of cucumbers, many cities and towns have a business similar to Metro Pedal Power that delivers to homes and families. Having lived in a few different spots across the United States, I've always managed to find ways to connect with farmers, from community-supported agriculture (CSA) boxes to farm drop-off services. CSA boxes, which bring consumers a selection of farm products throughout the season, can be wonderful for trying new produce. They can also be challenging, inundating you with an unfathomable number of beets or forcing you to research an unfamiliar variety of turnip. We've designed dishes such as the Cheddar Scallion Bread Pudding (page 113) and the Honey–Soy Butter Glazed Roots (page 108) to flexibly accommodate different vegetables, whether you're awash in roots, shoots, or leaves.

If you've got a farmers' market nearby, you have the luxury of leisurely browsing and chatting with your farmers. Beyond solely a shopping destination, farmers' markets are an excellent resource for learning what's in season and what's at peak deliciousness. You can pick up new recipes and suggestions for specific ingredients or discover the perfect new vegetable to try in your Golden Fortune Stir-Fry (page 100). And you can ask your farmer what vegetable might be good to tuck into a deep-fried fritter (page 104). Even without a green thumb, though, I can answer that for you: just about anything.

CARROT COCONUT SOUP

—— V, VV, GF, DF ——

This soup won over our hearts with its bold and festive color and hints of spice. With a creamy richness from the coconut milk, it's a warming and welcoming soup perfect for cooler days. We like it with the Middle Eastern herb and spice mixture *za'atar*, or you could try curry powder, *ras el hanout*, or ground Sichuan peppercorns. For garnish, you can swirl in a teaspoon of miso, drizzle with olive oil, or scatter with toasted croutons, chopped herbs, pickles—you name it.

Serves 4 as an appetizer or 2 as a main dish

1 scallion

1 tablespoon (13 g) olive oil or vegetable oil

1 pound (450 g) carrots, trimmed and sliced into ½-inch-thick coins (5 to 6 carrots)

3 cloves garlic, thinly sliced

One 1-inch piece fresh ginger, thinly sliced

1 teaspoon (4 g) za'atar

½ teaspoon (2 g) kosher salt, or to taste

2 cups (480 g) water or vegetable broth

1 cup (230 g) coconut milk

Splash of apple cider vinegar or rice vinegar

Thinly slice the scallion, setting aside the white and lighter green slices for the pot and the darkest green slices for garnish.

Heat the oil in a large saucepan over medium heat. Once the oil is shimmering, add the white and lighter green parts of the scallion, the carrots, garlic, ginger, za'atar, and salt to the pot. Cook, stirring occasionally, until everything starts to brown and give off a toasty aroma, about 6 minutes. Add the water and coconut milk, scraping up any browned bits from the bottom of the pot, which will help flavor the soup. Bring to a boil, then lower the heat and simmer until the carrots are softened, about 30 minutes.

Carefully pour the hot soup into a blender or use an immersion blender to puree until smooth. Explosion warning: If you're going the blender route, fill only halfway and make sure to remove the center of the blender cap so steam can escape. Use a thick tea towel to cover the hole instead and start on low speed, working your way up. Thin with water if needed.

Stir in the vinegar for brightness, taste, and add more salt as needed. Sprinkle with the reserved scallions or other toppings of your choice, then spoon into bowls and serve.

SPRING DUG PARSNIP SOUP

—— V, VVO, GF, DFO ——

This creamy spiced soup highlights the extra sweet, nutty flavor of "overwintered" parsnips. These roots remain in the frozen ground through the winter while cold temperatures convert the starch to sugar, then emerge in early spring as a delightfully sweet treat. If you're making this after early- to mid-spring, you may want to increase the honey to achieve a similar sweetness. For a more indulgent version, try a swirl of cream or whole yogurt at the end; for a vegan version, use olive oil and maple syrup. Either way, we highly recommend serving with warm, crusty bread for dipping. We also like to serve this dish chilled to preserve the goodness of the honey (heating destroys the enzymes of raw honey). (Also pictured: Charred Cabbage Salad, page 99 and Honey-Soy Butter Glazed Roots, page 108.)

NOTE: You can use pre-ground coriander and cumin instead of the whole seeds, but the flavors won't be as strong or aromatic.

Serves 4 as an appetizer or 2 as a main dish

1½ teaspoons (3 g) coriander seeds	1 teaspoon (3 g) smoked paprika	1 pound (450 g) spring-dug parsnips, peeled, halved lengthwise, and chopped (5 to 6 parsnips)	1½ tablespoons (30 g) honey (local and/or raw if possible) or maple syrup, or to taste
1 teaspoon (3 g) cumin seeds	2 tablespoons (1 ounce/30 g) unsalted butter or olive oil		Kosher salt
1 heaping teaspoon (2 g) Sichuan peppercorns	¼ small onion, diced	3 cups (720 g) vegetable stock or broth, or water	Freshly ground black pepper

Toast the coriander seeds, cumin seeds, and Sichuan peppercorns in a small skillet over medium heat until fragrant, about 2 minutes. Transfer to a spice grinder or mortar and pestle and grind to a fine powder. Sift through a fine-mesh strainer to remove large bits, mix with the paprika, and set aside.

Put the butter into a large saucepan over medium heat. Once the butter melts, add the onion and sweat until softened, about 3 minutes. Add the parsnips, spice blend, and stock. Bring to a boil, then lower the heat and simmer, mostly covered, until the parsnips are very tender and can easily be speared by a fork, about 30 minutes.

Carefully pour the hot soup into a blender or use an immersion blender to puree until smooth. Explosion warning: If you're going the blender route, fill only halfway and make sure to remove the center of the blender cap so steam can escape. Use a thick tea towel to cover the hole instead and start on low speed, working your way up. Thin with water if needed.

Drizzle with honey and season with salt and pepper, keeping in mind that you'll want more salt if you used water instead of stock. Spoon into bowls and serve.

HOT AND SOUR BORSCHT

——— V, VVO, GF, DFO ———

Our take on borscht always surprises people, with its vivid magenta hue and Asian flavors. We discovered there is a Chinese version of borscht similar to hot and sour soup, with cabbage and tomato instead of the classic Eastern European version with beets. Ours nods to both styles and also takes inspiration from Thailand and Korea, getting its "hot" from green chili curry paste and "sour" from kimchi or sauerkraut juice, but planting its foot firmly in the "borscht should have beets" camp. We like a dollop of something creamy on top, both to show off the vibrant color and to cool your mouth against the insistent attention of the green chili.

Serves 4 as an appetizer or 2 as a main dish

1 pound (450 g/about 3 medium) beets, trimmed

2 large carrots, cut into 2-inch pieces

1 medium onion, trimmed and sliced in half

2 cloves garlic

1½ tablespoons (20 g) olive oil

1½ teaspoons (5 g) kosher salt

2 teaspoons (8 g) neutral oil, such as canola or vegetable

1 tablespoon (15 g) green curry paste, or curry paste of your choice

½ cup (115 g) coconut milk

2 cups (480 g) water

1 tablespoon (15 g) kimchi or sauerkraut juice

Sour cream or plain yogurt, for garnish (omit if vegan or dairy-free)

Sprigs of dill, chopped scallions, or ribbons of sauerkraut, for garnish (optional)

Preheat the oven to 450°F (230°C).

Fold a large piece of aluminum foil in half and crimp the edges up so it makes a shallow tray. Place the beets, carrots, onions, and garlic on top, then drizzle with the olive oil and sprinkle with 1 teaspoon of the salt. Cover with another piece of foil and seal the edges, then place the packet onto a baking dish or baking sheet. Roast the vegetables until the beets can be pierced easily with a fork, about 1 hour and 15 minutes. Let the beets cool, then use the aluminum foil or a paper towel to push the skin off the beets and cut them into chunks.

Heat the neutral oil in a medium saucepan over medium heat until shimmering. Add the curry paste and cook for 2 minutes. Add the coconut milk and bring to a boil, then reduce the heat and simmer for 5 minutes, stirring occasionally. Remove from the heat and let cool slightly.

Transfer the curry sauce to a blender and add the beets, carrots, onion, garlic, water, the remaining ½ teaspoon salt, and the kimchi juice and blend carefully until smooth. Taste for seasoning, add more liquid, if needed, and serve hot or chilled with the toppings of your choice.

SMACKED CUCUMBER SALAD

—— V, VV, GFO, DF ——

This recipe infuses classic Chinese cucumber salad with a fresh, herby breath of spring. The smashing of the cucumber softens the edges and helps the pieces absorb more flavor; plus, it's fun to whack things. We encourage you to play around with the ingredients; if you can find some green garlic or garlic scapes, they're a wonderful seasonal substitute for the garlic cloves. If you don't have mint, try parsley or cilantro, and there's no reason you can't up the quantities of the herbs. Feel free to sprinkle on some crunch of your choice—at the restaurant, we like ours with salted Virginia peanuts. And like most things, it's excellent with some chunks of ripe avocado.

Serves 4 as a small snack, 2 as a side dish

SAUCE

1 clove garlic, or 1 stalk green garlic, or 2 stalks garlic scapes, minced

1 scallion, thinly sliced

Leaves from 4 sprigs mint, roughly chopped, plus more for garnish

2 tablespoons (30 g) rice vinegar

2 tablespoons (26 g) extra-virgin olive oil

1 tablespoon (15 g) sriracha

1½ teaspoons (8 g) soy sauce (substitute tamari if gluten-free)

Pinch of kosher salt, or to taste

OTHER INGREDIENTS

1 large English cucumber or 4 Kirby or Persian cucumbers

Additional herbs, diced scallions, peanuts, croutons, or breadcrumbs, for garnish (optional)

MAKE THE SAUCE

Combine all the sauce ingredients in a medium bowl or food processor and whisk or pulse to combine.

MAKE THE SALAD

Cut the cucumber(s) in half lengthwise and lay flat on cutting board, seed-side down. Vigorously smack the pieces with the flat side of a cleaver or a rolling pin until they start to splinter open. Cut lengthwise down the spines and then crosswise into bite-size pieces. Toss with the dressing, add salt to taste, and let sit in the refrigerator for at least 30 minutes or up to 24 hours. Taste and add more salt, if needed. Serve with your choice of garnishes.

MAGICAL KALE SALAD

—— v ——

We created this salad during the early days of the food truck to highlight great local greens and showcase our love for fried oozy eggs. The name comes courtesy of one of our early food truck regulars, Bianca, who got asked out on a date while eating it. Magical Kale Salad has become the go-to salad for many of our friends, as it's endlessly versatile and a big crowd pleaser. Try adding thinly sliced cabbage or Brussels sprouts, torn bread or crispy fried quinoa, crumbly blue cheese or ricotta salata, and anything else from anchovies to zucchini.

Another magical element of this salad is that it helps develop your seasoning skills. You combine kale, oil, and vinegar, then add a small pinch of salt to begin. Mix the dressing into the greens, then eat a piece of kale. Sprinkle a bit more salt on, mix, and eat another piece. Notice how the kale starts vaguely bitter and dry-tasting and then blooms with bright and enticing vegetal flavors. Continue, small pinch by small pinch, until it tastes so good you can't stop eating it. Let the salad sit while you prepare your eggs so the kale continues to get tender.

Serves 2 as a meal, 4 as a side dish

¾ cup (157 g) extra-virgin olive oil ¼ cup (60 g) rice vinegar or fresh lemon juice	1 large bunch kale—lacinato, curly, Red Russian, you pick! Kosher salt	½ cup (75 g) crumbled feta cheese, or more to taste ½ cup (40 g) Garlic Panko (page 14)	2 or 4 eggs, cooked using your method of choice (we like fried eggs with an oozy yolk)

Combine the oil and vinegar in a bowl or jar and whisk or shake to combine. Remove the stems from the kale—save them for Traditional-ish Pork Dumplings (page 62) or Leafy Greens Gratin (page 110)—and tear or chop the leaves into small ribbons. Place the leaves into a large bowl and drizzle on half the dressing. Season with a small pinch of salt, then massage the kale with your hands a bit to tenderize it.

Taste a piece of kale to check your dressing and seasoning. Slowly add more as necessary, tasting each time, until the kale is nicely coated with no extra dressing in the bottom of the bowl. It should taste deliciously green but not salty. You'll have some extra dressing left over—store in an airtight container in the refrigerator for up to a week and use on any salad.

Top the salad with the cheese, panko, and fried eggs and serve immediately.

BEEKEEPER'S SALAD

—— V, GF ——

This salad features the work of some hyper-local food producers in our city of Boston: bees. Bees can be a thriving part of urban agriculture as well as a vital part of the food system—their work pollinating crops is essential for many of the foods we eat as well as the food that feeds other animals in the food chain. This salad is both a celebration of bees and a study in contrasts, with the sweetness of honey against spicy, peppery greens and lightly bittersweet pops of bee pollen, all tossed with a cool, creamy yogurt dressing. There will be more dressing than you need for this salad; it tastes great on all things green and will keep in the refrigerator for up to three days.

Serves 4 as a side dish

YOGURT DRESSING (MAKES 1 CUP)

⅔ cup (150 g) plain whole yogurt

⅓ cup (80 g) buttermilk

2 teaspoons (10 g) fresh lemon juice

Kosher salt to taste

SALAD

4 ounces (about 8 cups loosely packed) arugula, watercress, or other peppery greens

¼ cup (25 g) crushed pecans or almonds

2 ounces (57 g) Manchego or aged cheddar cheese, shaved or thinly sliced

Leaves from a few sprigs of mint, chopped or torn

About 1 teaspoon (7 g) honey

About 1 teaspoon (8 g) bee pollen

MAKE THE DRESSING

Whisk together all the ingredients in a small bowl. The thickness may vary slightly depending on your brand of yogurt—aim for a creamy, tangy dressing that's thin enough to pour.

MAKE THE SALAD

Put the greens in a large bowl and pour ¼ cup of the dressing on top. Using your hands, carefully scoop and flip the greens until they are fully coated in the dressing. As our sous chef Emily says: *gently, gently, gently.*

Transfer the greens to a wide, shallow bowl and sprinkle with the nuts, then scatter the cheese and mint across the top. Delicately drizzle the honey on top in a very thin stream—the idea is to let the honey bead up on the herbs like dew on plants in the morning. Dust with the bee pollen and serve immediately.

CHARRED CABBAGE SALAD

—— V, GFO ——

We developed this salad as a winter alternative to the Magical Kale Salad (page 95), frantically buying up all the cabbage from our local farms as soon as kale went out of season. At first it merely swapped kale for cabbage, but we've taken it through many iterations and landed on this version, where tangy Fermented Black Bean Dressing sidles up cozily alongside smoky charred cabbage. Together, they stand up to an assertive blue cheese, with all that intensity cut by crisp cool chunks of apple. See if you can find a blue cheese local to you—we love Great Hill Blue from Buzzards Bay, Massachusetts. (As pictured on page 89.)

Serves 4 as a side dish

1 pound (450 g) red or green cabbage (about 1 small cabbage or ½ large cabbage)

1 medium sweet and crisp apple, such as a Honeycrisp, cored and diced

¾ cup (113 g) crumbled blue cheese, or to taste

¼ cup (50 g) Fermented Black Bean Dressing (page 17), or as needed

Kosher salt

½ cup (60 g) crushed peanuts or Garlic Panko (40 g) (page 14)

Remove any floppy outer leaves from the cabbage, slice it into 4 or 6 wedges, and cut out the core from each piece. Place cut-side down in a skillet (ideally cast-iron) large enough to hold all the pieces comfortably. Turn the heat to high and cook for roughly 3 minutes, until charred, aiming for a blackened surface. Use tongs to carefully flip the cabbage wedges and char the other side. Remove from the heat and let cool.

Place each cabbage wedge with a charred side down on a cutting board and thinly slice it. Put the sliced cabbage into a serving bowl, add the apple, cheese, and dressing and mix thoroughly. Season with salt. Taste for seasoning and add more dressing, salt, or cheese as desired. Top with crushed peanuts or Garlic Panko for crunch.

GOLDEN FORTUNE STIR-FRY

—— V, VV, GF, DF ——

When Irene developed this simple riff on a classic Chinese stir-fry, with its bright carrot coins and rich yellow corn, she gave it a classically auspicious Chinese name. While delicious with fresh seasonal produce, I find this recipe most valuable on rushed weeknights when it seems the sole residents of my kitchen are frozen corn and a lonely orphaned bag of carrots. We ate green beans dry-fried like this all the time growing up, and the charred, shriveled beans are packed with umami richness. The peanut sauce is so good that it'll make even the pickiest eater eat their greens. Or, in my daughter's case, eat a few green beans, then use the rest as a shovel to eat more sauce. Feel free to add in, leave out, or substitute other vegetables, but make sure they're chopped or sliced thinly (we use a mandoline) to maximize surface area and minimize cooking time.

Serves 4 as a side dish or 2 as a simple meal over rice or noodles

2 tablespoons (26 g) neutral oil, such as vegetable or canola	2 cups (300 g) trimmed green beans, cut into 2-inch pieces	1 medium carrot, thinly sliced into coins	3 tablespoons Peanut Sauce (page 18), or as needed
	1½ cups (225 g) sweet corn kernels, fresh or frozen and thawed	Kosher salt	Fresh torn cilantro leaves, for garnish

Heat the oil in a medium to large skillet or wok over high heat until shimmering. Add the green beans and cook, stirring occasionally, until they get a bit charred and wrinkly, 5 to 7 minutes. Add the corn and stir-fry for two minutes, then add the carrot coins and mix thoroughly. Cook for another 4 to 6 minutes, stirring every minute or so to allow new pieces to sear on the surface of the skillet.

Remove from the heat and transfer to a serving bowl. Season with salt. Add the peanut sauce and stir to coat. Taste and add more dressing or salt as desired. Add some torn cilantro leaves and serve immediately. Leftovers will keep for up to three days in the fridge.

ASPARAGUS TEMPURA

—— V, VV, DF ——

We once created a tempura dish as our submission to a springtime cooking competition on the Greenway, a stretch of public parks in downtown Boston and a regular parking spot for the food truck. Irene beer-battered and fried a haul of foraged fiddlehead ferns and won the cook-off! Since fiddleheads are only available for a few weeks in late spring and this dish is too good to eat once a year, after fiddlehead season we like to use asparagus for an addictively delicious snack. If you do score some fiddleheads, trim them and remove any brown spots before frying. Green beans are another great option, as would be another thinly sliced vegetable of your choice—it's hard to beat anything fried in a crunchy golden batter and dipped into homemade aioli! An important note: Make sure the beer in your batter is ice cold. Scientifically, it makes a better fryer batter (read J. Kenji López-Alt's *The Food Lab* to geek out on all the details). Practically, it is much more enjoyable to drink with your freshly fried tempura.

SPECIAL EQUIPMENT: thermometer, spider or slotted spoon, and large pot for deep-frying

Serves 4 to 6 as a snack

Neutral oil, such as peanut, for frying	½ cup (60 g) cornstarch	¾ cup (150 ml) beer, ideally a lager or pilsner, or soda water	Honey Walnut Mayonnaise (page 21) or Soy Aioli (page 23), for dipping
½ cup (60 g) all-purpose flour	1 teaspoon (3 g) kosher salt, or to taste	1 pound asparagus, trimmed and cut into 3-inch-long pieces	

Pour about 3 inches of oil into a large pot, such as a Dutch oven, making sure you have a few inches of clearance to the top of the pot. Heat the oil to 350°F (175°C).

Whisk together the flour, cornstarch, and salt in a medium bowl. Add the beer and stir until the batter comes together; it's OK if there are some globs of flour. Put the asparagus in the batter and use your hands to thoroughly coat each piece.

Line a plate with paper towels. Grab a few pieces of asparagus in one hand and let the excess batter drip back into the bowl. Carefully slip the battered asparagus into the hot oil, holding your fingers close to the surface to reduce splashing. Use the spider to separate stuck asparagus and continue to add asparagus until the surface is filled, leaving enough room around each piece to fry on its own. Cook until the batter reaches a pale golden blond, about 1½ minutes. Using the spider, transfer to the prepared plate and sprinkle lightly with salt. Repeat with the remaining asparagus.

Serve with mayonnaise or aioli for dipping.

NOTE: The oil from frying can be saved and used several times. Once the oil has cooled completely, strain and discard any solids and pour the filtered oil into a sealable container. Store in a cool, dry location. When the oil gets smelly or too murky to strain, seal in its original container or something that closes tightly, such as a soda bottle, and discard.

SWEET CORN FRITTERS

—— v ——

We started serving fritters on the truck because a) they're magical bites of fried deliciousness, and b) we wanted a side dish that could showcase seasonal ingredients throughout the year. We started with sweet corn in the summertime, moved to parsnip and apple in the fall, and experimented with smoked cheddar and scallion in the winter. Then our corn farmer, Four Town Farm in Seekonk Massachusetts, started freezing sweet corn at its peak to sell year-round. Since it was always the favorite child of the fritter family, we now run the sweet corn version whether there's blazing sun or three feet of snow outside.

NOTE: Masa harina is a corn flour treated with an alkaline solution in a process called nixtamalization, which softens the corn. It's used for tortillas, tamales, pupusas, and many other Latin American dishes. We like Maseca brand, which is available at many grocery stores.

SPECIAL EQUIPMENT: thermometer, spider or slotted spoon, and large pot for deep-frying

Makes about 24 fritters

¾ cup (100 g) masa flour, also known as masa harina or instant corn flour	⅓ cup (53 g) loosely packed brown sugar	2 teaspoons (6 g) kosher salt	2 large eggs
½ cup (65 g) corn flour	¼ cup (45 g) fine or medium cornmeal	1 cup (150 g) sweet corn kernels, fresh or frozen and thawed	½ cup (120 g) whole milk
½ cup (60 g) all-purpose flour	1 tablespoon (12 g) granulated sugar	4 tablespoons (2 ounces/55 g) unsalted butter, melted and cooled	Neutral oil, such as peanut, for frying
	2 teaspoons (8 g) baking powder		Sriracha Aioli (page 23)

Whisk together the masa, corn flour, all-purpose flour, brown sugar, cornmeal, granulated sugar, baking powder, and salt in a large bowl. Add the corn and mix until the kernels are fully incorporated. Whisk together the butter, eggs, and milk in a medium bowl, then add them to the dry ingredients and mix thoroughly.

Pour about 3 inches of oil in a large pot such as a Dutch oven, making sure you have a few inches of clearance to the top of the pot. Heat the oil to 375°F (190°C).

Line a plate with paper towels. Working in batches to ensure enough space, form the batter into balls about 1½ inches in diameter and carefully place into the hot oil. (In the restaurant, we use a disher to precisely scoop the right amount of batter directly into the oil; at home, we use our hands and get our fingers as close to the oil as possible to reduce oil splashes.) Fry, turning occasionally, until golden brown, about 3 minutes. Using a slotted spoon or spider, transfer to the prepared plate to cool.

These fritters are best served hot but are still excellent at room temperature. Serve with aioli or sriracha.

ROASTED MISO MAPLE POTATOES

—— V, VV, GFO, DF ——

This dressing combines two of our favorite flavors—miso for a rich earthy note and maple for a hit of sweetness and New England charm. Add in a bit of soy sauce for seasoning and touch of lemon juice for brightness and you've got a light yet surprisingly complex sauce that seems to melt into the potatoes. A garnish of Fried Shallots made while the potatoes roast, adds an extra-addictive oniony crunch that we can't get enough of.

While the dressing is pretty simple, the potato process might seem unnecessarily complicated. I learned this parboiling + shaking method from London friends with very particular opinions about Sunday roasts and the requisite potato accompaniment. The quick boil makes for a fluffy smooth texture inside the potato, and the shaking helps form an extra crispy crust. I find these textural differences to be extra important when the dish is all about potatoes. But if this seems like overkill, just chop, toss in oil, and roast away.

Serves 4 as a side dish

1½ pounds (675 g) potatoes, such as Yukon Gold, cut into 1-inch chunks (don't bother peeling)	1 tablespoon (17 g) miso, preferably white miso for a lighter flavor	1 teaspoon (5 g) soy sauce (substitute tamari if gluten-free)	2 tablespoons (26 g) olive oil
Kosher salt	1 tablespoon (13 g) neutral oil, such as canola or vegetable	1 teaspoon (5 g) fresh lemon juice	Fried Shallots (page 21) (or use store-bought), for garnish
1 tablespoon (20 g) maple syrup		3 tablespoons chopped fresh parsley	
		1 scallion, thinly sliced	

Preheat the oven to 450°F (230°C).

Put the potatoes and a large pinch of salt into a medium pot and add water to cover by a couple inches. Bring to a boil over high heat, then reduce the heat slightly and simmer until the potatoes can easily be speared with a fork, 10 to 12 minutes.

Meanwhile, whisk the maple syrup, miso, neutral oil, soy sauce, and lemon juice in a medium bowl. Set aside a large pinch of the parsley and scallion for garnish, then add the remainder to the bowl. Stir to combine and let the flavors mingle while the potatoes roast.

Strain the potatoes into a colander. Grab the colander and carefully shake it a few times, bouncing the potatoes up and down like they're on a trampoline. This gets rid of excess water and roughs up the outside of the potato chunks to create a better crust. Put the potatoes back into the pot and pour the olive oil over them. Using oven mitts or kitchen towels, grab the pot with both hands and give it another few shakes, tossing the potatoes so they get coated in the oil and a bit more shaggy and disheveled. Tip the potatoes onto a baking sheet, spread them out, and pop them into the oven for 20 minutes. Pull the sheet out and use tongs or a spatula to turn the potatoes over. Put them back in and roast another 15 to 20 minutes, until they have a good golden crust on at least a few sides. Remove from heat, let cool slightly, then mix in the miso maple sauce.

Serve immediately, topped with the reserved parsley, scallions, and a generous scattering of fried shallots.

HONEY–SOY BUTTER GLAZED ROOTS

—— V, GFO ——

This glaze has only four ingredients (okay, five if you count the water), but will surprise you with its depth of flavor and savory-sweet punch. We love using both the roots and the leaves of a vegetable—the spark of bitter greens is a lovely counterpoint to the sweetly glazed roots. Look for bunches of smaller root vegetables with the leaves still attached—think golf or billiard ball with tufts of healthy green leaves, not the trimmed softballs you sometimes see at the supermarket. For carrots, you want whole baby carrot bunches with leaves attached, not the shiny polished nuggets sealed inside a plastic bag.

Serve as a side dish with Red-Cooked Beef Stew (page 158) or Apple Hoisin–Glazed Pork Chops (page 14), or use to top Rice Porridge (page 164) or just a plain bowl of White Rice (page 31). (As pictured on page 89.)

Serves 4, as a side dish

2 bunches (about 1½ pounds/680 g) root vegetables, such as turnips (we especially like the Hakurei variety), radishes, beets, or small carrots

3 tablespoons (1½ ounces/40 g) unsalted butter

3 tablespoons (45 g) soy sauce (substitute tamari if gluten-free)

2 tablespoons (40 g) honey

1¼ cups (300 g) water, or more as needed

PREP THE ROOTS

Remove the leaves from the roots, run your knife through the leaves a few times, and set aside. Remove the stems and discard. Trim the roots. For smaller roots such as radishes or turnips, cut in half; for beets or larger turnips, cut in quarters or sixths depending on the size. Aim for all the roots to be roughly the same height in the pan.

Place the cut roots into a wide heavy-bottomed pan with 3-inch-high sides and add the butter, soy sauce, honey, and water. The roots should be mostly submerged; if not, add more water until they are.

Bring to a boil, then turn the heat down to low, cover, and simmer until you can insert a fork with little resistance but the roots are not yet tender,

about 15 minutes for beets and older turnips, and 10 minutes for spring turnips, radishes, or carrots. If you have a combination, put the beets in first; once they soften a bit, add the remaining vegetables.

Remove the cover and turn the heat up to medium-high. Bring the sauce to a fierce bubble and reduce to a thin layer in the bottom of the pan, about 15 minutes. Turn down the heat slightly if you see or smell signs of burning.

Add the reserved leaves and stir until everything is coated with the sauce. Turn the heat back down to low, cover, and simmer for 5 more minutes, then uncover and turn the heat up to medium. Simmer until the glaze is syrupy and barely coats the bottom of the pan, 5 to 7 minutes. Serve hot.

LEAFY GREENS GRATIN

—— V, GFO ——

During our days of volunteering at the Food Project urban farm, we often took home armfuls of vibrant, rainbow-toned chard. Our favorite way to use it up was this cheesy, crunchy gratin, made heartier with a Julia Child-inspired pantry staple we always have at hand: white rice. It's particularly useful for showcasing any leafy greens languishing in the fridge; not only will it rescue wilted leaves, but it's a perfect dish for utilizing otherwise underappreciated vegetable bits like the stems from kale, chard, and collards or the greens from beets or turnips. And it welcomes any melty cheese with open arms.

Serves 6 to 8, with sides

6 cups (1.35 kg) water

Kosher salt

½ cup (92 g) white rice

8 cups chopped (separated into stems and leaves) leafy greens (1 to 2 bunches kale, collards, turnip or beet greens, carrot tops, or other greens)

3 tablespoons (1½ ounces/40 g) unsalted butter or olive oil

1 medium onion, diced

2 cloves garlic, minced

2 tablespoons (14 g) all-purpose flour (substitute 1 tablespoon/7 g cornstarch to make it gluten-free)

1 cup (240 g) whole milk

1 cup (120 g) grated semi-firm melting cheese, such as cheddar, Gruyère, or fontina

Extra-virgin olive oil, for drizzling

Garlic Panko (page 14), for garnish (optional; omit for gluten-free)

Preheat the oven to 425°F (220°C).

Pour the water into a large pot, add a generous pinch of salt, and bring to a boil over medium-high heat. Add the rice and cook for 3 minutes. Add any chopped stems from the greens and cook for 2 minutes. Add the leaves, give the mixture a stir until everything is submerged, then boil for another 2 minutes. Meanwhile, set up a strainer over a bowl in the sink. When you drain the pot, pour the water into the bowl and reserve 1 cup of the vegetable water. Set the drained vegetables aside to cool.

Melt the butter in a large Dutch oven or other ovenproof heavy-bottomed saucepan over medium heat. Add the onion and garlic and cook, stirring occasionally, for 6 minutes, or until softened and lightly browned. Add the drained veggies and rice.

Turn the heat to low and stir to combine, then sprinkle the flour across the surface.

Add the reserved vegetable water and the milk and mix thoroughly, making sure there are no clumps of flour. Stir in ¾ cup (90 g) of the cheese and season with salt. Cook until the mixture has thickened slightly, 3 to 5 minutes. (You can make the dish up to this point, cool, cover, and refrigerate for up to 2 days before baking.)

Sprinkle with the remaining ¼ cup (30 g) cheese and drizzle with a generous pour of olive oil. Bake for about 20 minutes, until the top is golden brown and you want to attack it with a spoon.

Serve dusted with Garlic Panko, unless you've made the dish gluten-free.

CHEDDAR SCALLION BREAD PUDDING

——— v ———

If you've never had a savory bread pudding before, it's time to preheat the oven and get ready. Contrary to a dessert bread pudding, this dish encompasses both scallions and aromatics, plus a celebratory amount of cheese. With a rich, moist, eggy center, it's so satisfying that we've served this at countless food truck weddings, including my own. We stumbled onto this combination when we were sourcing local scallions and kept getting enormous bunches, as long as three feet. It's a fantastic way to use up scallion greens, but we'd say any member of the allium family—caramelized onions, ramps, garlic scapes, chives, leeks, and more—deserves an invitation to the party.

Serves 6 to 8, with sides

8 cups (1-inch cubes) bread, ideally a boule or baguette

4 cups (960 g) whole milk, or 2 cups (480 g) milk and 2 cups (480 g) heavy cream

2 large eggs

1½ cups (180 g) shredded sharp cheddar cheese, or another cheese of your choice

4 tablespoons (2 ounces /55 g) unsalted butter or olive oil, plus more for greasing the pan

4 cloves garlic, minced

1 medium onion, diced

Kosher salt

4 cups (240 g) thinly sliced scallions (2 to 3 bunches), or 2 cups chopped fresh herbs, or a combination

---

Preheat the oven to 350°F (175°C). Grease a 9 x 13-inch baking dish.

Put the bread into a large bowl. Whisk the milk and eggs together in a small bowl, then pour over the bread. Add 1 cup (55 g) of the cheese, mix thoroughly, and make sure all of the bread is submerged so it can soak up the milk.

Melt the butter in a large skillet over medium-low heat. Add the garlic and onion and a generous pinch of salt and cook until softened but not colored, about 5 minutes. Add the scallions and cook for another 4 minutes, or until tender but still bright green.

If you're using fresh herbs, no need to cook them; add them directly to the bread mixture. Remove the vegetables from the heat and let cool for a few minutes, then mix them into the bread mixture. Taste for seasoning (if you'd prefer not to try a mix with raw egg, season it after it's cooked).

Pour the bread and scallion mixture into the prepared pan. Spread it out evenly, then scatter the remaining ½ cup (55 g) cheese on top. Bake until the entire top is puffed and golden brown, about 1 hour. Serve hot or let cool and refrigerate—it makes phenomenal leftovers and transports well for picnics.

RICE, NOODLES, WHOLE GRAINS, AND OTHER FOOD IN BOWLS

When we were growing up, it was all about white rice in our house. Our family's medium-grain white rice lived in our kitchen cupboard in fifty-pound bags so large that two of us kids lifted them together to get them into the house, staggering under their weight. Every night, the rice cooker would flip from COOKING to KEEP WARM just in time for dinner, when everyone was expected to be in their chair and ready to eat at 6 p.m. Whether we were eating stir-fried pork or spaghetti and meatballs, in our Chinese-American household there was almost always white rice on the table.

These days, while we serve and eat plenty of white rice, we've gotten interested in exploring other grains, from brown rice to triticale, a wheat-rye hybrid. Through our friendship with the L'Etoile family, owners of Four Star Farms in Western Massachusetts, we've come to newly appreciate grains we knew only in other forms, like whole-grain rye berries. We started adding wheat berries—the intact kernel of wheat before it gets ground into flour—into salads, rice dishes, even desserts. We grind local grains into flour for crackers, sweets, and breads, and also sell the whole grains or flours in the mini market at our restaurant so we can spread the whole grain love.

Of course, we can't talk starches and bowls without discussing noodles. Noodles were ever-present in our childhood kitchen, primarily plain spaghetti, dried white Chinese Shanxi noodles, and instant ramen. All three of us kids mastered instant ramen at an early age, which we'd dress up with eggs or veggies or a splash of sesame oil. When I graduated from boiling to pan-frying, I delighted in my new cooking skills; I probably ate Pan-Fried Noodles (page 128) with soy sauce and sesame oil three times a week in high school. I'm happy to say that I have since incorporated both vegetables and other noodles like soba and rice sticks into my repertoire. All of these dried noodles will keep in your pantry for ages and are endlessly versatile, whether you're looking for something refreshing and cool like the Summer Noodle Salad (page 124) or something tangy and briny like the Soy Ginger Noodle Salad (page 126). If you're feeling adventurous, try making your own noodles from scratch (Biang Biang Noodles; page 131). It might seem intimidating, but with a bit of

practice, you'll be showing off an impressive skill in no time.

This chapter also includes the beloved Mei Mei curry bowls, which rotate throughout the year to feature what's in season. We might pair a green curry with radishes and bok choy in the spring, and toss some fall carrots and parsnips into a massaman curry once the weather gets chilly. Once you've prepared the chili paste with aromatics and sauces, you can easily swap in various vegetables, meats, and starches. As any farmer or gardener will tell you, "what grows together, goes together," meaning that produce grown at the same time tastes wonderful cooked together. Pair seasonal vegetables like tomatoes and corn or potatoes and cabbage with what you've got in the pantry and you've got all you need for a big bowl of curry (or a Red Curry Frito Pie; page 138) at any time of the year.

The same mix-and-match approach goes for Market Bowls (page 142), our substantial, meal-worthy salads stuffed with local grains, meats, cheeses, vegetables, and more. These meals are healthy, as they include a good mix of carbs, fat, and protein as well as a serious dose of colorful, nutrient-filled plants. Best of all, they're super easy to assemble. You'll need to plan ahead a bit with some strategic shopping or a bit of time in the kitchen. But once you have your ingredients ready, you'll be well prepared to create your own bowls in a matter of minutes.

We hope you'll enjoy these delicious bowls of food, whether you're aiming to cook a simple healthy meal or put a twist on an old favorite. You can even learn a new skill—we're willing to bet that noodle banging will seriously liven up your next dinner party!

FARMERS' MARKET FRIED RICE

—— V, GFO ——

Fried rice is a funny thing. Growing up with a pink-flowered plastic rice cooker ever-present on the counter, we made fried rice the way other kids make PB&J. With leftover rice, eggs, and scallions always available, fried rice was our go-to for breakfast or midnight snack. Now, in my own rice cooker–less home, fried rice is an event to be planned for, because dry leftover rice works best to absorb flavor and avoid clumps. If you don't have leftover rice on hand, be prepared for a bit of mushiness, but spreading it out to dry for 10 minutes goes a long way.

At home and at the restaurant, we feature seasonal vegetables (hence the recipe's name), so consider this recipe more a set of guidelines. A few important things to remember, no matter your ingredients: First, fried rice comes together quickly (except for that whole make-your-rice-a-day-ahead thing), so have your ingredients prepped and ready before you fry. Second, organize your ingredients by cooking time. Fresh peas and leafy greens only need a light sauté, while firmer ingredients like carrots or mushrooms need a few minutes to caramelize or soften. Feel free to move veggies from one category to another depending on how you like them cooked, and remember that thinner slices will cook faster. Last, the flavoring is up to you. I like my fried rice with the soy sauce and wine mixture below. Irene only uses salt. Andy prefers Frank's RedHot sauce.

Serves 4, with other dishes

SAUCE (feel free to customize—options include fish sauce, oyster sauce, toasted sesame oil, and a few pinches of sugar)

1 tablespoon (15 g) Shaoxing wine

1 tablespoon (15 g) soy sauce (substitute tamari if gluten-free)

1 tablespoon (15 g) rice vinegar

Kosher salt

SLOWER-COOKING VEGGIES

1 cup thinly sliced or diced carrots, parsnips, turnips, onions, shallots, leeks, asparagus, Brussels sprouts, leafy green stems (such as kale or chard), mushrooms, broccoli, cabbage, or green beans

QUICK-COOKING VEGGIES

1 cup bite-size pieces leafy greens (kale, arugula, spinach, chard, beet greens, turnip greens), whole bean sprouts, peas, or corn (fresh or frozen and thawed)

NO-COOKING VEGGIES AND HERBS

Sliced avocado, herbs such as mint, cilantro, or basil, any pickled vegetables

OTHER INGREDIENTS

3 tablespoons (40 g) neutral oil, such as canola

2 large eggs, lightly beaten

2 cloves garlic, minced

2 scallions, thinly sliced

One 1-inch piece ginger, minced

3 cups (375 g) cooked White Rice (page 14) (ideally leftover), crumbled into a large bowl to break up any clumps

(Continued)

Whisk together all the sauce ingredients in a small bowl.

Heat 1 tablespoon of the oil in a wok or large skillet (we like a large cast-iron skillet to maximize surface area) over medium-high heat until shimmering. Add the slower-cooking veggies and cook, stirring every minute or so, until they start to soften and lightly brown, 3 to 5 minutes. Transfer to a medium bowl and set aside.

Put the skillet back on the stove and add another 1 tablespoon of the oil. Heat until shimmering and add the beaten eggs. Let the eggs spread out and cook for about 10 seconds, then use a spatula to fold the eggs over themselves until just set (barely cooked and still soft), about 30 seconds. Transfer to the bowl with the cooked veggies and set aside.

Heat the remaining 1 tablespoon oil until shimmering. Add the garlic, scallions, and ginger and cook for about 30 seconds, then add the quick-cooking veggies. Stir-fry until wilted or softened, about 1 minute, then add the rice and stir to thoroughly mix. Spread the rice out in the skillet and fry for 1 minute, then stir and repeat 2 or 3 times so all of the rice gets heated and crunchy. Pour in the sauce and stir until the rice is lightly coated.

Add the eggs and slower-cooking veggies back into the pan and stir to combine, breaking up the eggs and reheating all the ingredients. Serve immediately, topped with any no-cook veggies or herbs you like.

NOTE: If you'd like to add meat, anything with its own fat such as bacon or ground beef (not the super-lean kind) can be cooked in the same skillet before starting the fried rice. Once cooked, remove the meat and set it aside, then start from the beginning, cooking the slower-cooking veggies in the fat and following the rest of the instructions from there. If you're using a leaner meat such as shrimp or chicken, you'll need an additional tablespoon or two of oil to start you off, then add more oil for the veggies. Add the cooked meat to the eggs to reheat before serving.

RYE FRIED RICE
WITH PICKLED CRANBERRIES AND HONEY SCALLION GOAT CHEESE

—— v ——

This unconventional fried rice features whole rye grains and black rice, instead of the white rice you know and love from Chinese restaurants. It's got chew and crunch, sweet and sour; it's tangy and nutty and all the things a fried rice never knew it could be. It has cheese! And fruit! Scoff you may, but try it and we daresay you'll change your mind about the untapped potential of fried rice.

The best part is that you don't have to worry about the intricate dance of finding rice at that perfect level of dryness for fried rice. Whole grains like rye and black rice come with their outer layer, called the bran, still attached and full of fiber and nutrients. The bran protects the grain like a tiny coat of armor, so they don't release starch and clump during frying. Side bonus: the bran keeps the grains from falling apart during cooking (they may split a little), so you can boil them vigorously like pasta. I cook the grains together to save a step, adding the rye first so it can cook a little longer. If you're combining other grains, just keep an eye on the suggested cooking times, or boil them separately. Try farro instead of rye, or barley instead of black rice, and it'll all be wholly inauthentic and totally awesome.

Serves 4 as a side dish.

HONEY SCALLION GOAT CHEESE

2 ounces (55 g) fresh soft goat cheese

¼ cup (60 g) heavy cream

1 teaspoon (7 g) honey

1 scallion, thinly sliced

Kosher salt

OTHER INGREDIENTS

⅓ cup (50 g) whole rye grains, also known as rye berries

⅓ cup (60 g) black rice

2 tablespoons (26 g) neutral oil, such as canola

2 medium carrots, peeled and sliced thinly into coins

1 scallion, thinly sliced

1 clove garlic, minced

¼ cup (50 g) Pickled Cranberries (page 24), drained

Kosher salt

MAKE THE HONEY SCALLION GOAT CHEESE

Using a wooden spoon or spatula, mix the cheese, cream, honey and half the scallions in a small bowl until smooth. Season with salt and set aside, leaving the remaining scallions for garnish.

COOK THE GRAINS

Bring a large pot of salted water to boil over medium-high heat. Add the rye, making sure the grains are covered by at least a few inches of water. Cook for 12 minutes, then add the black rice. Cook until both grains are tender, 30 to 40 more minutes. Drain well and spread out on a large plate to cool. (The grains can be done up to 5 days in advance, stored in a covered container in the refrigerator.)

COMPLETE THE DISH

Heat the oil in a large skillet (preferably cast-iron) over medium-high heat until shimmering. Add the carrot coins, scallion, and garlic and cook until lightly browned, 3 to 5 minutes. Add the rye and black rice and stir to combine, then spread the mixture out

across the skillet to maximize surface area for frying. Cook the grains until they get crunchy, about 5 minutes.

Remove from the heat and transfer to a bowl. Season with salt to taste. Mix in the pickled cranberries and top with the cheese mixture and the reserved scallions. Right before you take a bite, swirl the cheese so it melts into the rice and you get some in every bite.

SUMMER NOODLE SALAD
WITH GINGER GARLIC DRESSING

—— V, DF ——

Every year, during the hottest days of summer, our friends at Allandale Farm in Boston throw a party called Tomato Fest. Complete with hayrides, a cooking competition, and more urban farm fun, we always leave with pallets of juicy, sweet, height-of-summer tomatoes. After popping a few pints' worth straight into our mouths, we make dishes like this summer noodle salad, which combines the caramelized sweetness of roasted tomatoes with the fresh burst of ripe raw tomatoes. The pungent gingery garlicky dressing, brightened with both black vinegar and lime juice, riffs on a vinaigrette used in Chinese cuisine for cold dishes ranging from cucumber to chilled jellyfish. Drizzled here on prime summer produce, it's a fresh take on pasta salad that's perfect for your next picnic. If you are using out-of-season tomatoes, roast all of them.

Serves 4, with other dishes

DRESSING

One 1-inch piece fresh ginger, finely minced or grated on a Microplane

2 cloves garlic, finely minced or grated on a Microplane

2 tablespoons (30 g) soy sauce

2 tablespoons (26 g) extra-virgin olive oil

1½ tablespoons (22 g) fresh lime or lemon juice

1 tablespoon (20 g) honey

1 tablespoon (13 g) toasted sesame oil

1 teaspoon (5 g) black vinegar

Kosher salt

SALAD

1 pound (450 g) small summer tomatoes, cut in half or quartered if large

1 cup (150 g) corn kernels

1 tablespoon (13 g) extra-virgin olive oil

1 tablespoon (13 g) toasted sesame oil

Kosher salt

8 ounces (225 g) soba noodles

1 zucchini, spiralized or thinly sliced

1 cup (25 g) arugula or other salad greens

1 avocado, cut into chunks

1 scallion, thinly sliced

1 tablespoon (8 g) black or white sesame seeds

Preheat the oven to 400°F (205°C).

MAKE THE DRESSING
Combine all the ingredients in a small bowl, whisk, and let sit so the ginger and garlic have time to mellow while you make the salad.

MAKE THE SALAD
Put half the tomatoes, corn, olive oil, and sesame oil into a baking dish or baking sheet. Roast for 20 minutes, or until the vegetables are lightly charred.

Set aside to cool.

Bring a large pot of salted water to a boil and cook the soba according to the package instructions, about 4 minutes. Drain and rinse thoroughly under cold running water to stop the cooking. Put the soba into the large serving bowl with the roasted tomatoes and corn and add the fresh tomatoes, zucchini, arugula, avocado, and scallion.

Pour most of the dressing over the salad and toss, then taste and add more dressing as desired. Sprinkle with the sesame seeds and serve.

SOY GINGER NOODLE SALAD
WITH PICKLED CARROTS AND TOFU

—— V, VV, GFO, DF ——

I could eat this light, refreshing vegan noodle salad all day. Vinegary pickled carrots get tossed with mild, almost creamy bites of tofu, and the slick, briny strips of wakame provide ample personality to a base of chewy rice noodles. It's a great dish to make ahead for dinner parties, picnics, or your hungry future self. If you don't have Quick Pickled Carrots on hand, shred 3 medium carrots, toss with 1½ tablespoons seasoned rice vinegar, and let sit while you make the noodles.

Serves 4, with other dishes

½ ounce (14 g/about 2 heaping tablespoons) dried wakame or nori seaweed

Kosher salt

8 ounces (225 g) wide dried rice noodles, also known as rice sticks

Toasted sesame oil

1½ cups (150 g) Quick Pickled Carrots (page 24)

7 ounces (200 g) tofu, cut into bite-size cubes

¼ cup (50 g) Soy Ginger Dressing (page 16), or as needed

Crushed peanuts (optional)

Chopped fresh cilantro or parsley, or whole pea tendrils (optional)

Line a plate with paper towels. If using wakame, put it in a small bowl and add cold water to cover by 1 inch. Leave for 5 minutes to rehydrate, then drain and spread out on the prepared plate to dry. Slice any larger pieces into thin strips. If using nori, cut into bite-size pieces (pro tip: use scissors to cut the nori).

Bring a large pot of salted water to a boil. Add the rice noodles and cook according to the package directions. Drain, rinse briefly under cold water, and drain well. Put the noodles in a large serving bowl and toss with a little sesame oil to prevent sticking.

Add the seaweed, pickled carrots, tofu, and dressing to the bowl. Toss to coat the ingredients, adding more dressing if desired. If you can avoid refrigerating, do so; the rice noodles taste best at room temperature. Garnish with crushed peanuts and the chopped herbs of your choice.

PAN-FRIED NOODLES
WITH MARKET ROOTS AND GREENS

—— V, VV, DF ——

My favorite after-school snack as a teenager was this pan-fried noodle pancake, made with Shanxi noodles. The wide wheat noodles fry up into a chewy carbohydrate dream of just-boiled noodle surrounded by crispy golden crunch. You can also use thin Hong Kong–style egg noodles, which you may recognize as the flattened yellow nest topped with stir-fried seafood or meat in Chinese restaurants. Either way, you will have noodle and crunch, so you can't go wrong.

This dish is excellent to have in your repertoire, as it requires only a few pantry items and that one thing you bought at the farmers' market. Vegetables like turnips, radishes, and kohlrabi are a one-stop shop: the root, pan-fried in caramelized chunks, and the sautéed leaves offer contrasting textures and flavors. Consider adding ground pork, chicken, or scrambled eggs, or using Peanut Sauce (page 18) or Soy Ginger Dressing (page 16) instead of the sauce below. It's meant to be flexible, so enjoy tinkering with the ingredients. No matter what you include, it's a simple, satisfying dish that will fill all your crispy noodle cravings with a heap of vegetables to boot. (As pictured on page 165.)

Serves 2 as a main dish or 4 alongside other dishes

NOODLES

Kosher salt

8 ounces (225 g) Shanxi noodles or thin egg noodles, fresh if possible

2 tablespoons (26 g) neutral oil, such as canola, plus more for tossing the noodles

1 bunch roots with leaves, such as turnips or kohlrabi, or 1 bunch greens, such as kale or chard

SAUCE

2 tablespoons (30 g) soy sauce

1 tablespoon (15 g) Shaoxing wine

1½ tablespoons (25 g) Ginger Scallion Oil (page 18) with bits, or 1 tablespoon (13 g) toasted sesame oil

GARNISH

1 scallion, thinly sliced

MAKE THE NOODLES AND VEGETABLES

Bring a large pot of salted water to a boil over high heat. Add the noodles and cook according to the package directions. Drain, then rinse under cold water to cool. Toss with a splash of oil to keep the noodles separate and spread onto a plate.

If using roots, separate the vegetable into root, stalks, and leaves. Peel the roots if the exterior is tough and slice into thin bite-size pieces (the thinner they are, the faster they'll cook). Cut the leaves into short ribbons. Try the stalks; if they are fibrous or tough, discard them. If they aren't, cut them into bite-size pieces. If using greens, separate the leaves and stems. Cut the stems into bite-size pieces and the leaves into short ribbons.

Heat 1 tablespoon of the oil in a large skillet (nonstick if possible) or wok over medium-high heat until shimmering. Add the roots, stalks, and/or stems, and cook until lightly browned and tender. This could take 4 to 7 minutes, depending on what you have; just add thicker or sturdier items to the pan first. Transfer to a bowl, sprinkle lightly with salt, and add the remaining 1 tablespoon oil to the skillet. Add the noodles and spread them out to cover the full surface of the skillet. Cook until the bottom of the noodle pancake is golden brown and crispy, 4 to 8 minutes depending on the style of noodle. Using tongs and/or

a spatula, carefully turn over the noodles. Cook until golden brown on the bottom, another 4 to 6 minutes.

MAKE THE SAUCE

While the noodles are cooking, whisk together the soy sauce, wine, and ginger scallion oil. Once the noodles are browned on both sides, put the roots or stems back into the skillet and add the leaves on top. Pour the sauce mixture on top and stir-fry for 2 to 4 minutes until the leaves are wilted and everything is lightly coated in sauce. Remove from heat and taste for seasoning and sauciness. Sprinkle with scallions and serve immediately.

BIANG BIANG NOODLES
WITH CURRY YOGURT SAUCE

—— v ——

This dish of chewy, slippery hand-pulled noodles is one of my all-time favorites. *Biang biang mian* (*mian* meaning noodles) are allegedly named for the banging noise made when the noodle hits the table during the shaping process. Stretching the noodles as far as your arms go and flinging them around the kitchen is tons of fun and surprisingly achievable with this particular dough. After much trial and error and much noodle eating, we've settled on this flour blend, which includes one-third pastry flour. The lower protein content means lighter, more pliable dough, which means noodles you can bang with ease.

We serve these noodles with all sorts of sauces at the restaurant, including the popular curry yogurt sauce included here. But we also adore the simplicity of a classic Chinese sauce, especially if you have Chili Oil (page 20) or Ginger Scallion Oil (page 18) already waiting in your fridge. A large spoonful of either (or, ideally, both) with a splash of soy sauce and black vinegar and your sauce is ready in seconds.

Serves 4, with sides

1½ cups plus 1 tablespoon (188 g) all-purpose flour, plus more as needed	¾ cup (75 g) unbleached or whole wheat pastry flour ⅔ cup plus 1 teaspoon (165 g) water	1 teaspoon (3 g) kosher salt, plus more for the cooking water Neutral oil, such as canola, or nonstick cooking spray	Yogurt Curry Sauce (recipe follows), or another sauce of choice, for serving

Combine the flours, water, and salt in the bowl of a stand mixer with the dough hook attached. Mix on the lowest setting until the dough starts to come together into a ball. Turn off the mixer and knead the ball a few times in the bowl to pick up any stray floury bits. If it sticks to your hands, mix in 1 teaspoon of all-purpose flour at a time until it no longer sticks. If it's too dry, add 1 teaspoon of water at a time until all the flour is incorporated.

Turn the mixer back on, set it to a low-medium speed, and mix for 10 minutes, or until the dough is soft and smooth. Lay a piece of plastic wrap on a flat surface and lightly oil or spray it. Remove the dough from the bowl, place it on the plastic, and wrap tightly. Let rest for at least 1 hour or overnight

in the refrigerator. If refrigerating, let it sit at room temperature for 30 minutes before making the noodles.

When you're ready to make the noodles, bring a large pot of salted water to a boil, then lower the heat and cover it while you shape the noodles. Clear yourself some counter space and set up a baking sheet to hold the pulled noodles. Remove the dough from the plastic wrap and shape the dough into a flat 10 by 10-inch square with your fingers or a rolling pin. Using a sharp knife, slice the square into 10 parallel strips, each about 1 inch wide.

One at a time, grab a strip loosely by the ends and slowly stretch it into a long noodle, lightly flicking your wrists and slapping it against the countertop as you widen your hands as far as they go. Lay the pulled pieces down on the baking sheet so the noodles are separated and don't stick.

When you're ready to cook, uncover the pot and turn the heat back to high. Once the water is bubbling, carefully add as many noodles as fit comfortably. Stir so the noodles don't stick to each other, then boil for about 1 minute, until the noodles float to the surface and are cooked through and tender. Drain and repeat with the remaining noodles, then add the sauce of your choice and serve immediately.

CURRY YOGURT SAUCE

Makes about 1 cup

4 tablespoons (2 ounces/55 g) unsalted butter

One 2-inch piece ginger, minced

½ small onion, diced

3 cloves garlic, minced

1 tablespoon (10 g) fermented black beans, rinsed and chopped

3 tablespoons (50 g) almond butter

1½ teaspoons (3 g) curry powder

½ cup (113 g) plain whole yogurt

1½ teaspoons (10 g) honey

Kosher salt

Melt the butter in a small saucepan over medium heat. Add the ginger, onion, garlic, and fermented black beans and cook until the vegetables are softened, about 5 minutes. Add the almond butter and curry powder, stir to combine, then turn the heat down to low and simmer 5 minutes.

Put the yogurt into a bowl with some extra room. Temper it by adding a spoonful of the hot almond mixture and stir to combine. Slowly warm up the yogurt with a few more spoonfuls of the almond mixture, then add the bowl of yogurt to the saucepan. Using a wooden spoon or a spatula, mix the yogurt in thoroughly, then add the honey. Taste for seasoning and adjust as necessary. Immediately pour over the biang biang noodles.

Leftovers will keep for up to 3 days in the refrigerator. To reheat, slowly (to keep the yogurt from curdling) warm the sauce up on the stovetop. This sauce is also great with roasted vegetables.

SPRING GREEN CURRY
WITH HALLOUMI

—— V, GFO ——

We change our curry seasonally at Mei Mei, varying the spices, toppings, and especially the vegetables. We've included two of our favorites here, but no need to feel bound by the seasonal names. Switch out the veggies according to what's available: lightly sauté zucchini and summer squash when it's sweltering out or roast winter root vegetables like sweet potato and parsnip during blizzard season. My favorite part is the halloumi, a semi-hard sheep's milk cheese that gives off delightful squeaky bursts of salt when you bite into it. The high melting point means that you can sear it until crispy on the outside, and there are few things I love more in the world than fried cheese. I recommend frying extra to snack on while you cook—in my experience, it's the only way to ensure you have any left for the curry. Serve over steamed rice or a whole grain and garnish with Cabbage Pickles (page 25), Fried Shallots (page 21), microgreens, pea shoots, or the herbs of your choice.

(Continued)

Serves 4 to 6 over steamed rice

CURRY SAUCE

¼ cup (52 g) neutral oil, such as canola

⅓ cup (85 g) green curry paste, or curry paste of your choice

3 cloves garlic, minced

One 2-inch piece fresh ginger, minced

½ medium onion, minced

Two 13.5-ounce (400 g) cans unsweetened coconut milk

2 tablespoons (30 g) soy sauce (substitute tamari if gluten-free)

1 tablespoon (20 g) honey

1 teaspoon (5 g) sherry vinegar

Kosher salt

OTHER INGREDIENTS

8 ounces (225 g) halloumi cheese, cut into bite-size chunks

8 ounces (225 g) zucchini or summer squash, cut into bite-size chunks

1 cup (150 g) corn kernels, fresh or frozen and thawed

8 ounces (225 g) firm tofu, cut into bite-size chunks (optional)

MAKE THE SAUCE

Heat the oil in a medium saucepan over medium heat until shimmering. Add the curry paste and cook, stirring, for 2 minutes. Add the garlic, ginger, and onion and cook until softened, about 4 minutes. Add the coconut milk, bring to a simmer, and cook for 10 minutes to let the flavors get to know each other. Remove from heat and stir in the soy sauce, honey, and vinegar. Season with salt. At this point, the sauce can be cooled and refrigerated if you're not planning to eat it soon.

Heat a skillet over medium-high heat and fry the halloumi until golden brown on 2 sides, 1 to 2 minutes per side. Set aside and try not to eat all of it. If needed, warm the curry sauce in a medium saucepan, then add the zucchini, corn, and tofu, if using, and simmer for 5 minutes. Add the fried halloumi, stir to combine, then remove from the heat. Taste for seasoning and serve over rice with the garnishes of your choice.

HARVEST MOON CURRY

—— V, VV, GFO, DF ——

Our cold weather curry features root vegetables and poblano chile for a touch more spice. We roast the veggies to get crispy browned sides, but you can also steam or boil them. This hearty and satisfying vegan curry will keep you warm on a wintry day, and it also welcomes meat such as shredded chicken, pulled pork, or cooked ground beef. Serve over steamed rice or a whole grain and garnish with Cabbage Pickles (page 25), Fried Shallots (page 21), microgreens, pea shoots, or the herbs of your choice.

Serves 4 to 6 over steamed rice

ROASTED VEGETABLES

1 pound (450 g) root vegetables, such as potatoes, carrots, or parsnips, cut into 1-inch chunks

1 tablespoon (13 g) olive oil

Kosher salt

CURRY SAUCE

¼ cup (52 g) neutral oil, such as canola

⅓ cup (85 g) red curry paste, or curry paste of your choice

1 clove garlic, minced

One 1-inch piece fresh ginger, minced

2 tablespoons (20 g) diced poblano chile

½ medium onion, minced

Two 13.5-ounce (400 g) cans unsweetened coconut milk

2 tablespoons (30 g) soy sauce (substitute tamari if gluten-free)

1 tablespoon (20 g) maple syrup

1 tablespoon (15 g) ketchup

1 teaspoon (5 g) rice vinegar

Kosher salt

ROAST THE VEGETABLES

Preheat the oven to 400°F (205°C).

Scatter the vegetable chunks onto a baking sheet and drizzle with the oil. Toss with your hands to coat and sprinkle with a generous pinch of salt. Roast until the largest pieces can be easily pierced by a fork, about 30 minutes.

MAKE THE SAUCE

Heat the oil in a medium saucepan over medium heat until shimmering. Add the curry paste and cook, stirring, for 2 minutes. Add the garlic, ginger, chile, and onion and cook until softened, about 4 minutes. Add the coconut milk, bring to a simmer, and simmer for 10 minutes to let the flavors get to know each other. Remove from the heat and stir in the soy sauce, maple syrup, ketchup, and vinegar. Season with salt. At this point, the sauce can be cooled and refrigerated if you're not planning to eat it soon.

Add the cooked root vegetables, taste for seasoning, then serve over rice with the garnishes of your choice.

RED CURRY FRITO PIE

—— V, GF ——

We should be up front here: Frito pie is not really a pie. It's usually made with chili, cheese, and other tasty stuff tucked into a snack-size bag of Fritos, as if nachos came in a handy carrying case (hence its other moniker, the walking taco). In Boston we've become a bit famous for Frito pies. We top them with Kung Pao Chicken Dip (page 154) or Cumin Lamb (similar to page 168) and serve them at craft beer festivals, fundraiser pop-ups, and benefit galas. Here we include our Summer Sunset Curry variation, but we also encourage you to try the curries on pages 133, and 137. along with other toppings. The sauce can easily be multiplied for feeding a party or to serve half as Frito Pie and half over rice and veggies for a simple dinner.

Serves 4 as a hearty snack

SUMMER SUNSET CURRY SAUCE

1½ tablespoons (20 g) neutral oil, such as canola

¼ medium onion, minced

One 1-inch piece ginger, minced

2 cloves garlic, minced

1 tablespoon (16 g) red curry paste, or curry paste of your choice

10 ounces (285 g) coconut milk

1½ teaspoons (8 g) tomato paste

1 teaspoon (7 g) honey

1 teaspoon (5 g) apple cider or rice vinegar

Kosher salt

TO SERVE

4 snack-size bags of Fritos

½ cup (60 g) shredded cheddar cheese

¼ cup (60 g) sour cream

2 tablespoons (15 g) minced red or white onion (optional)

8 sprigs cilantro, roughly chopped

MAKE THE CURRY SAUCE

Heat the oil in a medium saucepan over medium-low heat until shimmering. Add the onion, ginger, garlic, and curry paste and cook, stirring occasionally, until the vegetables soften, about 6 minutes.

Add the coconut milk and tomato paste and turn up the heat to medium. Bring to a simmer and simmer for 8 minutes, stirring occasionally, reducing the heat slightly if the sauce starts to boil furiously. Remove from heat, stir in the honey and vinegar, and season with salt.

ASSEMBLE THE FRITO PIES

Divide the curry sauce among the 4 bags of Fritos. Sprinkle each bag with an equal amount of cheese, sour cream, onion, and cilantro and serve immediately.

WHEAT BERRY SALAD
WITH PICKLED CRANBERRIES AND GOAT CHEESE

——— v ———

This recipe is a riff on a wheat berry salad we sold in the early days of the food truck, with some delightful additions (creamy goat cheese, yes please) and strategic subtractions (candy thermometer, no thank you) for a home kitchen. For someone who took a long time to come around to sweet and savory together, my obsession with this salad is a testament to how creatively it dances around that relationship. There are pickled cranberries, with a jammy intensity and an acidic kick. There's the miso honey dressing, which starts with sugar on your tongue but is backed up by strong umami undertones. Add a tinge of bitterness from the charred scallions and the nutty chew of the wheat berries and this salad hits all the right notes.

Serves 4 or more

½ cup (100 g) dried wheat berries or other whole grain, or about 1½ cups (150 g) cooked grains

2 medium sweet potatoes

6 scallions or spring onions

4 ounces (115 g/about 8 cups loosely packed) Boston or Bibb lettuce, or another leafy green of your choice, leaves torn into bite-size pieces

½ cup (100 g) Pickled Cranberries, drained (page 24)

4 ounces (115 g) fresh goat cheese

⅓ cup (75 g) Miso Honey Dressing (page 17), or more to taste

Kosher salt

Preheat the oven to 450°F (230°C).

MAKE THE WHEAT BERRIES AND SWEET POTATOES

Put the wheat berries in a small pot and cover with several inches of water. Bring to a boil over high heat, then reduce the heat slightly and simmer until fully cooked and tender, 45 to 60 minutes depending on the variety. Drain and let cool.

While the wheat berries are cooking, wrap the sweet potatoes in aluminum foil, place them on a baking sheet, and place the sheet in the oven. Bake until a fork can easily be inserted into the thickest part with no resistance, 45 minutes or more depending on the shape and size of the sweet potatoes. Remove from the oven and let cool, then peel and discard the skins and cut into 1-inch pieces.

CHAR THE SCALLIONS

Thinly slice the white parts of the scallions and cut the greens into ½-inch-long pieces. Toss both the whites and greens into a small skillet, turn the heat to high, and char them, about 4 minutes (you can toss in the garlic for the dressing to save a step). If you are using precooked wheat berries from the fridge, add them to the skillet in the final minute with a small glug of olive oil to reheat and add some extra crunch.

TO SERVE

Put the lettuce leaves into a wide, shallow bowl and scatter the sweet potato chunks, wheat berries, and charred scallions on top. Dot with the pickled cranberries and chunks of goat cheese, then drizzle with the dressing. Toss lightly, then add additional dressing or salt as needed.

OUR FAVORITE MARKET BOWLS

Our food truck serves these delightful bowls stuffed with pasture-raised meats, fresh greens, colorful veggies, local cheeses, and whole grains. We call them Market Bowls and love how well they translate to making convenient, flexible, satisfying-yet-healthy meals at home. I like to take a weekend day or a free night to cook a big pot of grains, pickle some veggies, or pick up ready-to-go items at the store. Midweek, it's a pleasure to find these building blocks stashed in the fridge; toss the grains and pickles with browned sausage, a just-opened can of beans, and some cooked beets. Add a sprinkle of cheese and greens and dinner is on the table in ten or fifteen minutes. Whether you

choose one of our favorites below or design your own, we think you'll love these bowls. Layered with brown rice, bulked up with other whole grains, or dotted with roasted potatoes, these hefty dishes are enough for a meal or an impressive side dish. And there might even be enough left over for lunch tomorrow too.

NOTE: All of the whole grains can be prepared like pasta. Bring a large pot of salted water to a boil and add your grains (the water should cover the grains by at least 3 inches). Cook according to the package directions—although taste often toward the end, as cook times can vary—then drain.

Grains	Barley	Rye
	Brown rice	Triticale
	Farro	Wheat berries
	Quinoa	
Greens	Arugula	Mesclun mix
	Kale	Spinach
	Lettuce	Spring greens
Veggies	Corn kernels	Root veggies such as carrots, beets, turnips, or radishes (roasted, boiled, pickled, or raw)
	Mushrooms (sautéed, roasted, marinated)	
	Roasted potatoes or winter squash, sliced	Tomatoes, diced
		Zucchini or summer squash, sliced
Proteins	Bacon bits	Ham, sliced
	Beans	Sausage, crumbled or sliced
	Chicken, shredded	
	Chickpeas, cooked	Tofu, cubed
	Chorizo, crumbled	
Cheese	Blue cheese, crumbled	Mozzarella cheese, shredded
	Cheddar cheese, shredded	
	Feta cheese, crumbled	Queso blanco, shredded
	Goat cheese, crumbled	
Other Fun Stuff	Apples, sliced	Fresh herbs
	Blueberries or strawberries	Hummus
		Kimchi
	Dried cranberries	Pesto
Crunch	Almonds	Garlic Panko (page 14)
		Peanuts
	Fried Shallots (page 21)	Sunflower seeds

THE HEIWA MARKET BOWL, AKA THE LIL' KIM CHI

— V, VV, GFO, DF —

We named this bowl for our favorite organic tofu, made in small batches by an adorable family up in Maine. It's bright and zingy from pickled carrots and kimchi and anchored by hearty whole grains and mild tofu. We use kimchi made with an assortment of veggies from the biodynamic farm Hawthorne Valley, as it offers more textural variation and acidity than the typical cabbage-only version.

Serves 2 as a main dish or 4 as a side

2 cups (300 g) cooked whole grains such as wheat berries or brown rice

2 cups (40 g) arugula or other salad leaves

4 ounces (115 g) firm tofu, cut into bite-size cubes

½ cup (50 g) Quick Pickled Carrots (page 24)

½ cup (75 g) kimchi

½ cup (60 g) crushed peanuts

⅓ cup (80 g) Creamy Garlic Peanut Dressing (recipe follows), or dressing of your choice

Combine all the ingredients except the dressing in a large bowl and toss to mix thoroughly. Add most of the dressing, stir to coat, then taste and add more dressing as desired.

CREAMY PEANUT GARLIC DRESSING

1½ cups (315 g) neutral oil, such as canola

½ cup (120 g) rice vinegar

¼ cup (60 g) unsweetened, creamy peanut butter

1½ tablespoons (18 g) sugar

3 cloves garlic, finely minced or grated on a Microplane

Kosher salt, to taste

Put all the ingredients in a bowl, blender, or food processor and whisk or blend to combine. Season to taste, then store in an airtight container in the fridge for up to two weeks.

THE FOUR STAR MARKET BOWL

—— GFO, DF ——

This dish highlights the offerings of Four Star Farms, a multigenerational family grain farm in Northfield, Massachusetts. The L'Etoile family grows a wide variety of whole grains that we use all over the menu, from cornmeal in our Sweet Corn Fritters (page 104) to the triticale (a wheat-rye hybrid) in this bowl. With cranberry dressing, sausage, and potatoes, this bowl has echoes of Thanksgiving, lightened up with arugula and a bit of sparkle from the pickled cranberries.

Serves 2 as a main dish or 4 as a side

2 cups (40 g) arugula or other salad leaves

1½ cups (180 g) roasted potato chunks

1 cup (150 g) cooked whole grains such as triticale or wheat berries or brown rice

1 cup (120 g) sausage crumbles or 2 cooked sausages, cut into chunks

2 tablespoons (25 g) Pickled Cranberries (page 24)

2 tablespoons (20 g) Fried Shallots (page 21)

⅓ cup (80 g) Tangy Cranberry Dressing (recipe follows) or dressing of your choice

Combine all the ingredients except the dressing in a large bowl and toss to mix thoroughly. Add most of the dressing, stir to coat, then taste and add more dressing as desired.

TANGY CRANBERRY DRESSING

1½ cups (315 g) neutral oil

½ cup (120 g) rice vinegar

½ cup (120 g) Cranberry Sweet and Sour Sauce (page 104)

Kosher salt, to taste

Put all the ingredients in a bowl or blender and whisk or blend to combine. Season to taste, then store in an airtight container in the fridge for up to two weeks.

THE NARRAGANSETT MARKET BOWL, AKA THE CHORIZARD

—— GF ——

Despite its Pokémon-inspired nickname, this bowl honors our favorite cheese makers, family-owned Narragansett Creamery in Rhode Island. We've used their gold medal–winning Salty Sea Feta since the first days of the food truck, and its creaminess stands up beautifully to crumbles of smoky spiced chorizo. This bowl gets its heft from a big scoop of warm heirloom beans, making it comforting, protein-packed, and gluten- and grain-free.

Serves 2 as a main dish or 4 as a side

2 cups (40 g) arugula or other salad leaves

1½ cups (180 g) crumbled cooked chorizo

1 cup (175 g) cooked beans of your choice

½ cup (75 g) crumbled feta cheese

½ cup (50 g) Quick Pickled Carrots (page 24)

2 tablespoons (20 g) Fried Shallots (page 21)

⅓ cup (80 g) Umami Apple Dressing, or dressing of your choice

Combine all the ingredients except the dressing in a large bowl and toss to mix thoroughly. Add most of the dressing, stir to coat, then taste and add more dressing as desired.

UMAMI APPLE DRESSING

1½ cups (315 g) neutral oil, such as canola

½ cup (120 g) Apple Hoisin Sauce (page 16)

½ cup (120 g) rice vinegar

Put all the ingredients in a bowl or blender and whisk or blend to combine. Season to taste, then store in an airtight container in the fridge for up to two weeks.

DOUBLE AWESOME CHINESE FOOD

THE PIGGERY MARKET BOWL

—— GFO, DF ——

We love our friends at The Piggery, so it's no surprise that this bacon-laden bowl is named for Brad and Heather. Their small-scale USDA-certified processing facility and butcher shop, where Irene worked during college, makes it possible for us to serve great quality, pasture-raised meat from animals that lived a good life on their farm and partner farms. We know because they send us photos of Brad rolling around in the hay with the pigs, and it's hard to tell who's having more fun.

Serves 2 as a main dish or 4 as a side

2 cups (40 g) baby spinach or other salad leaves

1 cup (150 g) cooked whole grains, such as barley or brown rice

1 cup (100 g) bacon bits

¾ cup (120 g) cooked sliced beets

⅓ cup (80 g) Soy Ginger Dressing (page 16), or dressing of your choice

2 tablespoons (10 g) Garlic Panko (page 14) (omit if gluten-free)

Combine all the ingredients except the dressing in a large bowl and toss to mix thoroughly. Add most of the dressing, stir to coat, then taste and add more dressing as desired.

FROM THE PASTURE

For as long as we've been interested in food as a family, Irene has been particularly passionate about animal welfare and humanely raised meat. But a very hands-on experience helped cement that commitment . . . we'll let her tell you in her own words.

Irene: I can pinpoint the moment I decided to serve exclusively pasture-raised meat at Mei Mei: the day I butchered a 250-pound pig on my childhood dining table. My journey of exploring meat production—talking to farmers, visiting slaughterhouses, and reading about ethical eating—had started some time before then, while I was at college in upstate New York. But it wasn't until I stood with a bone saw in hand, staring a bit dumbfounded at an enormous animal—nearly twice my size—sprawled dead in my mom's kitchen that it really sunk in. I was about to cut a pig into small pieces and eat it. As I, along with our opening co-chef Max, started to break down the pig, I felt a deep desire to honor the life of this animal by using every last bit of its body for food. We spent the day sawing, packaging, salting, freezing, roasting, and boiling until we each fell into bed exhausted, with a Five-Spice Pork Shoulder (page 172) roasting overnight in the oven.

The experience—and the months afterward eating pork chops and prosciutto—gave me a profound appreciation for all the work of farmers and butchers that is invisible to most consumers. Since that day in early 2012, I've tried to hold on to that feeling while navigating the complex world of purchasing meat. At Mei Mei, we take our meat seriously. The restaurant exists to serve food that is seriously delicious, but with a serious commitment to sourcing and buying meat the most responsible way we can. That means spending our money to support a food system where animals spend their lives in comfortable, natural surroundings and where the people who raise them are respected and fairly compensated. Where animals are slaughtered carefully and humanely and prepared for consumption without distasteful and dangerous industrial farming practices.

Sourcing meat according to these standards—which we refer to as pasture-raised—is more challenging and more expensive than following the status quo of factory farmed meat, especially as our businesses have grown. I visit farms, request certifications, and ask loads of questions of our farmers and distributors. To afford this higher-quality meat, we use the overlooked and unloved bits and try to serve meat as part of balanced dishes—as a treat or a heavy garnish rather than the main event. It helps that this ethos is grounded in a historically Chinese approach to cuisine, one that you see in many other countries as well. Where meat is a luxury for the average citizen, dishes such as stir-fries and fried rice allow the starch or vegetable to be the star.

This chapter will offer suggestions on how to cook with ethically raised meat. And don't worry—you won't have to butcher a whole pig! A good starting place is finding organic, antibiotic-free, hormone-free meat in your supermarket. Buying this meat tells your local grocery store that these products will sell, and they'll stock more of them. It's often easiest to find ground meat at higher standards, so you could try the Lion's Head Meatballs (page 160) with grass-fed ground beef or the Cumin Lamb Shepherd's Pie (page 168) with ground lamb. Another option is to try something similar to what you usually buy, but less processed; if your go-to is boneless pork loin, try a bone-in chop for Apple Hoisin–Glazed Pork Chops (page 164).

We've also designed this chapter to help you shop a bit more affordably at natural foods grocers, or, even better, farmers' markets, where the meat is typically held to a high standard. Rather than buying the choicest (read: most expensive) cuts, try a cheaper option like beef chuck in Red-Cooked Beef Stew (page 158), or any cut of pork ribs for Maple Chili Garlic Rib Tips (page 171). When cooking for a crowd, try large-format pork cuts like shoulder and belly. With time, these humbler areas of the pig are transformed into the most succulent, flavorful meat, like Roast Pork Belly (page 166) and Five-Spice Pork Shoulder (page 172).

We celebrate a tiny bit when we hear a customer

say "I'm typically vegetarian, but I'll order meat at Mei Mei because I know where the meat came from and that it was ethically raised." Or when we hear that our chicken farmer can afford to invest in a new henhouse because we committed to buying all their chicken wings for a season. We hope you find these recipes worth celebrating too.

KUNG PAO CHICKEN DIP

—— GFO ——

One could argue that this recipe epitomizes our food philosophy: Chinese food + cheese = winning. When you can't decide whether to order takeout Chinese or pizza, this dish gives you the best of both worlds. Spicy, gooey, and downright addictive, it entices guests to crowd around the snack table at parties, or calls you to consume a bowl by yourself on the couch. We serve it with house-made crackers at the restaurant, but also love crostini or a hunk of crusty bread and a generous helping of peanuts.

Serves 4 as an appetizer

¼ cup (60 g) black vinegar (substitute rice vinegar if gluten-free)

2½ tablespoons (30 g) sugar

2 tablespoons (30 g) soy sauce (substitute tamari if gluten-free)

2 tablespoons (30 g) Apple Hoisin Sauce (page XX) [[ms 38]] or store-bought hoisin sauce

2 tablespoons (30 g) Shaoxing wine

2 tablespoons (26 g) toasted sesame oil

2 tablespoons (14 g) cornstarch

1 teaspoon (4 g) Sichuan peppercorns, ground in a mortar and pestle or spice grinder

1 tablespoon (13 g) neutral oil, such as canola or vegetable

4 scallions, thinly sliced

3 cloves garlic, minced

One 2-inch piece fresh ginger, minced

1 tablespoon (5 g) chili flakes, or more as desired

¾ cup (90 g) shredded cheddar cheese

½ cup (110 g) cream cheese

¼ cup (60 g) buttermilk, or 1 tablespoon whole milk plus 3 tablespoons plain yogurt (preferably whole)

8 ounces (225 g) chopped or shredded chicken

¼ cup (30 g) crushed peanuts (optional)

Whisk the vinegar, sugar, soy sauce, hoisin sauce, wine, sesame oil, cornstarch, and Sichuan peppercorns together in a medium bowl.

In a medium saucepan, heat the oil over medium-high heat until shimmering. Add 3 of the scallions, garlic, and ginger and cook until softened and fragrant, about 2 minutes. Turn the heat down to low, then add the chili flakes and cook for 1 minute. Add the vinegar mixture and cook, stirring, for another minute to combine and thicken. Add the cheddar cheese, cream cheese, buttermilk, and chicken and stir to incorporate all the ingredients. Cook, stirring occasionally, until the cheese is melted, then taste for seasoning. Transfer to a serving dish and sprinkle with the remaining scallion slices and crushed peanuts. Serve with crostini, crackers, or bread.

SALT AND PEPPER CHICKEN WINGS

—— GF, DF ——

Everyone knows salt and pepper. These two familiar companions stand guard by our stoves, perch contentedly on restaurant tables, and even come handily packaged with your takeout utensils. They're usually not the main show, but sometimes these two deserve to be in the spotlight. In Chinese cuisine, particularly Cantonese, the pairing shines as the primary flavor profile of restaurant dishes like Salt and Pepper Shrimp (page 180) and salt and pepper pork chops. Toasted with a selection of peppercorns including tingly Sichuan peppercorns, they are beguilingly addictive on these baked chicken wings, an easy home version of our deep-fried restaurant dish. You can stick with just the salt and pepper dusting or toss or serve with Cranberry Sweet and Sour Sauce (page 15), Apple Hoisin Sauce (page 16), or another sauce of choice.

Serves 4 to 6, with other dishes

1 tablespoon (10 g) Toasted Salt and Peppercorns (page 20)	2 pounds (900 g) chicken wings	Scallions, thinly sliced, for garnish (optional)

Preheat the oven to 400°F (205°C). Cover a baking pan with aluminum foil, then place a wire rack on top. If you don't have a rack, just use the foil or a piece of parchment paper.

Toss the chicken wings in half of the salt and pepper mixture, then place on the rack or directly on the covered pan. Set the remaining spice mix aside for additional seasoning later.

Bake the wings for 40 to 50 minutes, until fully cooked and crispy. If you're not using a rack, use tongs to flip the wings about halfway through. Try a chicken wing to see if it needs more salt and pepper and adjust the seasoning as necessary, then serve immediately, with scallions and your choice of sauce, if using.

RED-COOKED BEEF STEW
WITH WHOLE GRAINS AND WINTER GREENS

—— DF ——

This stew is based on a popular dish from our early food truck days, Chinese red-cooked beef, braised with an extensive array of sauces and spices. We've added whole grains and winter greens to make this a hearty one-pot meal, a classic made new again with subtle hints of star anise, fennel, and Sichuan peppercorns. Or you can just make the beef to top porridge, fold into tacos, or roll into dumplings. No matter how you eat it, we think it's a warm and welcoming bite of happiness.

Serves 4

RED-COOKED BEEF

1 tablespoon (13 g) neutral oil, such as canola

1 pound (450 g) boneless beef short ribs, or other stew meat such as chuck, cut into 1-inch chunks

¼ cup (60 g) Shaoxing wine

¼ cup (60 g) soy sauce

2 tablespoons (30 g) black vinegar

4 cups (960 g) beef or chicken stock or broth, or water

½ medium onion, diced (leave whole if making only the beef)

One 2-inch piece ginger, cut in half lengthwise

2 cloves garlic

4 scallions

3 star anise

1 tablespoon (12 g) sugar

½ teaspoon fennel seeds, ground

½ teaspoon Sichuan peppercorns, ground

OTHER INGREDIENTS

1 cup (150 g) whole grains, such as wheat berries, farro or barley

3 carrots, sliced into ½-inch-thick coins

2 or more cups hearty greens, such as kale, savoy or napa cabbage, chard, or collards, cut into bite-size pieces

1 scallion, thinly sliced, for garnish

Fresh cilantro leaves, for garnish

MAKE THE BEEF

Heat the oil in a Dutch oven or heavy-bottomed stockpot over medium-high heat until shimmering. Add the beef to the pot and sear until well browned on two sides, 7 to 10 minutes.

Add the wine, soy sauce, and vinegar and stir, scraping the bottom of the pot to release any browned bits. Add the stock, onion, ginger, garlic, scallions, star anise, sugar, fennel seeds, and Sichuan peppercorns. Increase the heat and bring to a boil, then reduce the heat to low, partially cover, and simmer for about 1 hour, checking every so often to make sure the stew maintains a low, steady simmer, until the beef is cooked through

and tender. Using tongs, carefully remove and discard the ginger, scallions, garlic, and star anise. (If you would like to make the beef only, remove the onion, then use the tongs or a fork to pull apart the beef. Submerge the beef into the sauce and simmer for about 15 minutes, until the sauce thickens slightly. Remove from the heat and let the beef cool in the sauce to soak up more liquid.)

Add the grains and carrots and simmer over medium-low heat, checking regularly to make sure there is still ample liquid covering the grains; if necessary, add ¼ cup stock or water and repeat as needed. Depending on your choice of grain, it might take 30 minutes to 1 hour or more until they are fully cooked. We start

checking at the time printed on the package, and allow extra time because the grains aren't being cooked at a full boil. Once cooked to your liking, add the greens and stir vigorously until they are wilted and mixed into the beef and grains. Add more liquid and stir again over the heat if you'd like a soupier stew.

Serve topped with the scallion and cilantro. The stew will keep, refrigerated, for up to 5 days.

LION'S HEAD MEATBALLS
WITH STEWED EGGPLANT

This recipe evokes both its namesake, Shanghai dish (supposedly named for the image of lions' heads poking out of a broth), and the Italian-American classic of meatballs simmered in tomato sauce. Ingredient-wise, they're basically an international trade agreement, flavored with umami-rich Asian ingredients while borrowing the more Western trick of adding dairy for moisture and tang. We swap out tomatoes for another member of the nightshade family, one that's also eager to soften during a long simmer on the stovetop: the humble eggplant. The eggplant replaces and then one-ups the typical Chinese cornstarch slurry; it likewise thickens and adds body, but with more texture and the inarguable bonus of being a full serving of vegetables.

Serves 4, with sides

SAUCE

3 tablespoons (40 g) toasted sesame oil

2 tablespoons (26 g) neutral oil, such as canola

1 scallion, thinly sliced

1 pound (450 g) eggplant, typically 2 Japanese or Chinese eggplants or 1 large eggplant, cut into 1-inch chunks

1 clove garlic, thinly sliced

1½ cups (360 g) chicken broth or water

2 tablespoons (30 g) soy sauce

1 tablespoon (15 g) Shaoxing wine

1 teaspoon (4 g) sugar

Kosher salt

MEATBALLS

1 pound (450 g) ground beef, preferably not too lean

1 large egg

¼ cup (55 g) plain whole yogurt

3 tablespoons (15 g) panko, or other breadcrumbs

1 tablespoon (15 g) Apple Hoisin Sauce (page 16) or store-bought hoisin sauce

1 tablespoon (15 g) ketchup

2 teaspoons (10 g) soy sauce

1 teaspoon (5 g) fish sauce

½ teaspoon (2 g) ground white pepper

¼ teaspoon (1 g) kosher salt, or to taste

MAKE THE SAUCE

Heat the oils with the scallion in a medium to large pot or Dutch oven over medium heat. Once the scallion starts to sizzle, after about 6 minutes, add the eggplant and stir to coat it in oil. Cook for about 10 minutes, until the eggplant starts to soften, then add the garlic, chicken broth, soy sauce, wine, and sugar. Bring to a simmer and cook, partially covered, until the eggplant is very soft, about 20 minutes.

MAKE THE MEATBALLS

While the eggplant is cooking, combine the meatball ingredients in a large bowl and mix thoroughly. Form into meatballs roughly 1½ inches in diameter. Heat a large skillet over medium-high heat and fry a tablespoon of the meat to check for seasoning and adjust as needed. Carefully place the meatballs into the skillet and brown on all sides, about 4 minutes. Remove from the heat and set aside. (Note: The meatballs won't be cooked all the way; if you want to eat them without the sauce, make sure to use a heatproof skillet or transfer them to a baking dish

and bake in a preheated 350°F/175°C oven for 5 to 7 minutes, until cooked through.)

Use a wooden spoon or tongs to mash any large pieces of eggplant, then carefully transfer the meatballs to the eggplant stew. Turn the heat down to medium-low and simmer for another 20 minutes or so, until the meatballs are cooked through and the eggplant is so tender that it's spoonable. Season with salt, then serve on their own or ladle over White Rice (page 14), Rice Porridge (page 31), or a plain bowl of noodles.

SESAME SSAM JANG
BRISKET LETTUCE WRAPS

—— DF ——

Our badass ex-neuroscientist sous chef Emily developed this recipe, our take on the Korean dipping sauce *ssamjang*, which means "sauce for wraps." Made from a fermented soybean paste called *doenjang* (similar to miso) and the more familiar chili paste *gochujang*, it's spicy, sweet, salty, and in-your-face. Taste it and you'll marvel at the funkiness and depth of flavor; I often find myself sneaking spoonfuls while preparing this recipe, like a kid with a bowl of brownie batter.

Ssamjang is often served with grilled beef or pork; once we happened to have an enticingly fatty cut of brisket around and fell for that. We braise it with beer and nestle it into a pile of onions that slowly cook into a jammy tangle at the bottom of your pot. After hours in the oven, the meat emerges tender and triumphant, the sauce thick and potent, and it's all clamoring to be joined by something light, bright, and crunchy and enfolded in a refreshing lettuce hug.

Serves 6 to 8, with some White Rice (page 14)

BRISKET

⅓ cup (90 g) doenjang or miso

⅓ cup (70 g) toasted sesame oil

¼ cup (80 g) gochujang

2 tablespoons (40 g) honey

1 tablespoon (15 g) Chinese sesame paste or tahini

3 cloves garlic, minced

2 tablespoons (26 g) neutral oil, such as canola

One 3-pound (1.3 kg) beef brisket

3 medium onions, thinly sliced

1 cup (200 g) beer

FOR SERVING

Lettuce, for wrapping (we like Bibb or Butter lettuce)

Cabbage Pickles (page 25), another pickle of your choice, or Apple-Scallion Salad (page 37)

Soy Aioli (page 23), or another sauce of your choice

Preheat the oven to 325°F (160°C).

Mix the doenjang, sesame oil, gochujang, honey, sesame paste, and garlic in a small bowl. Heat the neutral oil in a Dutch oven or a large heavy-bottomed pot for which you have a lid over medium-high heat. Once the oil is shimmering, add the brisket and sear on both sides until well browned, about 5 minutes per side.

Using sturdy tongs or a large fork, carefully transfer the brisket to a large plate or platter. Add the onions and beer to the pot, using a wooden spoon to scrape up any browned bits from the bottom of the pot. Cook the

onions for about 10 minutes, until they are browned and softened. Turn off the heat, then place the brisket on top of the onions along with any juices from the plate.

Take the wooden spoon and smear the paste all over the top of the brisket. Cover the pot, place it in the oven, and cook, basting every so often, for 3 to 4 hours. Add more beer as needed (or even better, drink the rest of it). Pull the pot out of the oven, slice the beef against the grain, and return to the pot to soak up any juices. Let cool slightly and lay on a platter alongside lettuce, pickles, and sauce for people to assemble their own lettuce wraps.

APPLE HOISIN–GLAZED PORK CHOPS

—— GF, DF ——

Sometimes it's fun to explore obscure and ignored cuts of meat; other times, we crave a classic cut like a beautiful, well-raised pork chop. We treat it like a great steak—high heat and flip often—but at about half the price, so you can put the money toward high-quality, sustainably farmed meat. Knowing you've got great meat, we're all about cooking to medium-rare so it's juicy and pale pink, and not doing too much to it. Whether you've already made Apple Hoisin Sauce or you whisk together a quick and dirty five-ingredient version, it gives the pork a touch of sweetness and an intriguingly earthy edge to the charred crust. Serve with sides such as Stir-Fried Greens (page 48) or Wheat Berry Salad (page 140). (Also pictured: Pan-Fried Noodles with Market Roots and Greens, page 128.)

NOTE: If you don't have Apple Hoisin Sauce, you can whisk together 2 tablespoons applesauce, 2 tablespoons Chinese sesame paste or tahini, 1 tablespoon soy sauce (use tamari if gluten-free), 1 tablespoon black vinegar, and 2 teaspoons honey.

Serves 2 to 4, with sides

½ cup (120 g) Apple Hoisin Sauce (page 16)	**OTHER INGREDIENTS** Two 6- to 8-ounce (170- to 225-g) bone-in pork rib or blade-end chops, about 1½ inches thick	Kosher salt	1 tablespoon (13 g) neutral oil, such as canola or vegetable

Season the pork chops all over with salt, then place them in a large resealable bag with half of the sauce. Marinate for at least 30 minutes or up to 12 hours in the refrigerator, reserving the remaining sauce for later.

When you're ready to cook, remove the chops from the bag and pat with paper towels to remove extra sauce. Heat the oil in a large skillet, preferably cast-iron, over high heat until starting to smoke. Using tongs, carefully add the chops to the pan and cook until the bottoms are lightly browned, about 1 minute. Flip and brown the other side, then continue to turn once every minute or so until both sides are well browned and lightly charred, 7 to 9 minutes. Turn down the heat slightly if it is smoking too much. We cook to 130 to 135°F (54 to 57°C) on an instant-read thermometer; go a bit longer if you prefer a more well-done chop. Using tongs, carefully remove the pork chops from the pan and let rest for at least 5 minutes before slicing. Set the remaining sauce on the side for dipping and serve immediately.

ROAST PORK BELLY

—— GFO, DF ——

Roast pork belly, from pigs we butchered ourselves, was one of our first food truck specials. We grew up eating the belly on its own, in fatty chunks cut from slabs hanging enticingly in Cantonese restaurant windows. On the truck, we tucked the belly into elaborate buns with house-made bread, pickles, and sauces. With all those fancy trappings, plus a long marinade and slow roast, the pork belly got too complicated to have on the menu every day, so we started running Pork Bun Sundays at a truck spot a few blocks from our childhood home. This is all to say that yes, this is a bit of a long-winded recipe, but it's worth it when you slice into the rich, luscious belly topped with a layer of crispy golden crackling. It's spectacular on its own, or check out the Five-Spice Pork Shoulder (page 172) for details on how to put together your own fancy buns. If you miraculously have leftovers, use them to top Dan Dan Noodles (page 45) or Rice Porridge (page 31), or fry the chunks on all sides for pork belly "croutons."

Serves 4 to 6, with sides

MARINADE

4 cloves garlic, minced

1 tablespoon (20 g) honey

1 tablespoon (15 g) soy sauce (substitute tamari if gluten-free)

1 tablespoon (15 g) Shaoxing wine

1 tablespoon (10 g) kosher salt

½ teaspoon (2 g) five-spice powder

½ teaspoon (2 g) ground white pepper

OTHER INGREDIENTS

3 pounds skin-on pork belly (look for flatter pieces that will cook more evenly)

1 cup (160 g) kosher salt

MARINATE THE PORK

Rinse the pork belly in water and pat dry on all sides with paper towels. Use the tip of a sharp knife to poke an array of shallow holes across the skin. I aim for roughly one notch per square centimeter, jabbing the knife so it pierces the skin but ideally doesn't reach the meat.

Combine the marinade ingredients in a small bowl and stir to make a paste. Smear the marinade onto the meat side and thoroughly coat the entire surface. Place the belly into a flat pan so the marinated side rests on the bottom and let sit for at least 1 hour on the counter, or up to 24 hours in the fridge (the longer you let it marinate, the more flavorful it will be, but even 1 hour is enough time in a pinch).

COOK THE PORK

Preheat the oven to 375°F (190°C).

Press the pork flat and wipe the skin dry again with paper towels; a dry surface will give you maximum crispiness. Place the pork onto a large piece of aluminum foil with a few inches of foil on each side. Fold up the foil along the sides of the belly so the belly is in a tight foil box with at least a 1-inch border of foil along the top. Carefully pour the salt over the skin and spread it over the top of the belly, using the foil as a barrier to keep the salt from falling down the sides. Place the foil box onto a baking sheet or baking dish and place it in the oven.

Roast for 30 minutes, then lower the oven temperature to 300°F (150°C) and roast for 2 hours. Take the pan out of the oven; the salt should have baked

into a hard layer that can easily be lifted off the belly. Remove the salt crust and discard. If the crust didn't completely harden, just push the salt off and brush the pork to remove any remaining salt. Use tongs to lift the pork out of the foil box and set aside. If there's a lot of pork fat, strain it through a coffee filter and refrigerate it to make Whole Wheat Steamed Buns (page 175). Discard the foil and cover the baking sheet with a new piece of foil, then put the pork belly back on the pan. If one side of the pork is much thicker than the other, use crumpled pieces of aluminum foil to prop up the thinner section so the skin is as flat as possible. Position a rack about 8 inches from the broiler.

Turn the broiler to low; if your broiler doesn't have a low setting, move the rack down one level. Put the pork in the oven and let the heat slowly crisp up the skin. I leave the door open so I can easily check on the pork, rotating the pan if necessary to heat the top as evenly as possible. This process can take 10 to 15 minutes depending on your oven and the pork thickness; taking it slow allows the skin to lighten and puff up without burning.

Remove from the oven and let cool slightly, then use a sharp knife to cut the belly into chunks. Serve immediately.

CUMIN LAMB SHEPHERD'S PIE

—— GFO ——

This dish infuses the Midwestern shepherd's pie of our childhood with the traditional Northwest Chinese combination of toasty cumin paired with the light gaminess of lamb. I serve it often at home—my Scottish-Chinese husband goes wild for the union of mashed potatoes and Chinese spices. It's great for dinner parties—make it in advance and pop it into the oven to reheat before serving. If you can't get good lamb, use ground beef, and feel free to experiment with winter veggies or use up the contents of a CSA box; we've tried parsnips, carrots, taro root, squash, and beets in all sorts of pairings. If you cook the veggies long enough that they get a little caramelized, it's a joy to unearth a nugget of crunch and sweetness amid the heat of the chilies and the buzzy numbing of the Sichuan peppercorns. It's got enough spice that my husband complains, but he wolfs it down anyway. Serve with sides such as Magical Kale Salad (page 95).

Serves 4 to 6, with sides

ROASTED VEGETABLES

2 tablespoons (26 g) neutral oil, such as canola

1½ pounds (675 g) root vegetables (such as 5 carrots and 2 parsnips), cut into 1-inch pieces

CUMIN LAMB

1 tablespoon (13 g) neutral oil, such as canola

1 pound (450 g) ground lamb

½ medium onion

One 1-inch piece ginger, minced

2 cloves garlic, minced

1 tablespoon (5 g) chili flakes, or toasted diced chile of your choice

1½ tablespoons (12 g) all-purpose flour (substitute 1 tablespoon/7 g cornstarch if gluten-free)

⅓ cup (80 g) Shaoxing wine

⅓ cup (80 g) water

¼ cup (60 g) soy sauce (substitute tamari if gluten-free)

2 teaspoons (10 g) fish sauce

2 tablespoons (15 g) finely chopped fresh cilantro leaves and stems

1½ tablespoons (10 g) ground cumin

1 tablespoon (4 g) Sichuan peppercorns, ground

MASHED POTATOES

Kosher salt

3 large russet potatoes (about 1½ pounds/ 675 g)

¼ cup (60 g) heavy cream

¼ cup (60 g) milk (or omit the cream and use ½ cup/120 g milk)

4 tablespoons (2 ounces/55 g) unsalted butter

Freshly ground black pepper

ROAST THE VEGETABLES

Preheat the oven to 350°F (175°C).

Put the root vegetables on a baking sheet, drizzle with the oil, then toss and fully coat them with the oil. Roast until tender and lightly caramelized but not mushy, 35 to 45 minutes.

MAKE THE CUMIN LAMB

While the root veggies are roasting, heat the oil in a large skillet or Dutch oven over medium heat until shimmering. Add the lamb and cook, stirring to break it up, until browned (it doesn't have to be fully cooked, as it will simmer with the sauce later), 3 to 5 minutes. Remove from the heat and transfer to a medium bowl. If a lot of fat has accumulated, transfer to a heatproof container until only a light sheen is left in the pan.

Return the pan to medium heat, add the onion, ginger, garlic, and chili flakes, and cook until softened and fragrant, about 3 minutes. Add the flour and stir to combine. Turn the heat down to medium-low and add the wine, water, soy sauce, and fish sauce. Stir and scrape the bottom of the pan for a minute to deglaze, then return the lamb to the pan and simmer until the lamb is cooked through and the sauce has reduced slightly, 10 to 15 minutes. If you feel up to multitasking, this is a good time to start the mashed potatoes.

Remove from the heat, add the cilantro, cumin, and peppercorns, and stir to combine, then taste for seasoning and spice level. (This is the point where you need to try hard not to eat the whole mixture straight out of the pan. Do your best. No one will notice a few bites missing, though).

Stir the roasted root vegetables into the lamb mixture. If you used a skillet, transfer the lamb and veggie mixture to a large casserole dish; otherwise leave it in the Dutch oven.

MAKE THE POTATOES

Bring a large pot of salted water to a boil. Meanwhile, cut the potatoes into 1-inch pieces and rinse under cool water to get rid of excess starch. Add to the boiling water and cook until the potatoes can be easily pierced by a fork, about 15 minutes.

Drain the potatoes, then put them back in the hot pot. Add the cream, milk, and butter and mash with a potato masher or large fork. Season with salt and pepper, keeping in mind that the lamb mixture will be well seasoned and flavorful.

Once both the mashed potatoes and lamb mixture are ready, spoon the mash on top of the lamb and vegetables. Serve immediately, or let cool and store, covered, in the refrigerator for up to 2 days. Reheat in the oven at 350°F (175°C) for 30 to 45 minutes.

MAPLE CHILI GARLIC RIB TIPS

—— DF ——

Irene: While I was in college, I worked at The Piggery, a family-run farm and butcher shop business in Trumansburg, New York, that sells traditional pasture-raised meats. While slicing ham and breaking down chickens for customers, I noticed that the rib tips—the lower end of the spareribs—never sold well. I get why some people avoid them—they can be a bit chewy and they've got cartilage that doesn't line up straight like the rest of the ribs. But they're meatier and more marbled (as I see it, more fat = more awesome). And if you're willing to put in a little work, it's well worth the effort, as many barbecue enthusiasts swear. After failing to convert many customers, I made Heather, one of the owners, an offer. Mei Mei would commit to purchasing a certain amount of rib tips every week, and she'd give us her best price. Turned out to be a win-win for everyone!

If you can't find tips (try calling a local butcher shop), this recipe is interchangeably excellent with baby back ribs, spareribs, or St. Louis cut ribs. No matter what part of the rib you get, rib eating should always be a messy, finger-licking, face-smearing, napkin-using affair, so you might as well enjoy it.

Serves 4 to 6, with other dishes

¼ cup (60 g) Apple Hoisin Sauce (page 16) or store-bought hoisin sauce	¼ cup (70 g) chili garlic sauce	1 tablespoon (15 g) soy sauce	2 pounds (900 g) rib tips or ribs of choice
	1½ tablespoons (30 g) maple syrup	1 tablespoon (15 g) black vinegar	

Preheat the oven to 300°F (150°C).

Combine the hoisin sauce, chili garlic sauce, maple syrup, soy sauce, and vinegar in a medium saucepan. Bring to a simmer over medium-low heat and cook, stirring occasionally to prevent crusting on the bottom of the pan, until the sauce is thick and sticky, about 15 minutes. Meanwhile, wrap the rib tips in aluminum foil and place on a baking sheet or in a baking dish. Cook for 1½ hours, or until the ribs are tender and juicy. Remove from the oven and discard the foil.

Arrange an oven rack so it's 5 inches from the heat element and switch the oven to broil. Line a baking sheet with aluminum foil. Generously brush the ribs on both sides with sauce, then place them on the sheet. Broil for about 3 minutes on each side, until the ribs are crackling and glistening and starting to char. Serve with the remaining sauce on the side for dipping.

FIVE-SPICE PORK SHOULDER
WITH WHOLE WHEAT STEAMED BUNS

Irene: *The River Cottage Meat Book,* by Hugh Fearnley Whittingstall, helped change the way I think about meat. Mei sent it to me from England, where Hugh is a celebrity chef/farmer/food advocate, right when I was starting to meet and learn from farmers in upstate New York. I urge you to buy his book, both for Hugh's respectful, inspiring, and informative words on good meat and the uniformly superb recipes, like this family favorite pork shoulder roast. Hugh uses a whole pork shoulder on the bone (eleven to eighteen pounds) and calls the dish Donnie Brasco, because you can put it in an oven overnight and *fuhgeddaboutit.*

While his version magnificently feeds a whole party, we've tweaked the ingredients and scaled it down a bit for smaller groups. Rather than a full twenty-four-hour roast, this eight(ish)-hour version allows you to sleep in a bit and pop the pork in the oven in the morning. You'll have a lovely porky smell in the kitchen all day, with plenty of time to make pickles, sauces, and Whole Wheat Steamed Buns (or pop out to the store to buy them), and then it's ready just in time for dinner. Leftovers are top-notch with eggs as breakfast hash, made into tacos or sandwiches, or served atop Rice Porridge (page 31).

Serves 6 to 8, with sides

One 2-inch piece fresh ginger, minced	1½ teaspoons (5 g) kosher salt	1½ cups (360 g) orange juice	Sriracha Aioli, Soy Aioli (page 23), or mayonnaise mixed with sriracha
4 cloves garlic, minced	One 4- to 6-pound (1.8- to 2.75-kg) boneless skinless pork shoulder (also known as a pork butt or Boston butt), or 5 to 7 pounds (2.25 to 3 kg) bone-in skinless pork shoulder	**FOR SERVING**	Cranberry Sweet and Sour Sauce (page 15) or Apple Hoisin Sauce (page 16) or store-bought hoisin sauce
2 tablespoons (40 g) maple syrup		Whole Wheat Steamed Buns (recipe follows)	
1 tablespoon (15 g) soy sauce		Quick Pickled Carrots (page 24; we also like this with thin slices of pickled cucumber or rhubarb)	Thinly sliced scallions
1 tablespoon (6 g) five-spice powder			

Preheat the oven to 450°F (230°C).

Combine the ginger, garlic, maple syrup, five-spice powder, and salt in a small bowl or food processor and stir or pulse to mix thoroughly. Pat the pork dry with paper towels, then rub it all over with the spice mixture. Put the pork into a roasting pan or Dutch oven with the fat facing up. Pour the orange juice into the pan around the shoulder and place in the oven.

Roast for 30 minutes to brown the shoulder, then lower the oven temperature to 265°F (130°C) and roast for 6 to 8 hours more, opening the oven every so often to baste the shoulder with the juices. I like the way the meat starts to fall apart after about 8 hours, but if you're slightly short on time, you can cook it less (depending on the size of your shoulder)—the texture may be more sliceable than shreddable. Carefully pull the pot out of the oven. Using tongs and a large fork (or a knife and cutting board if needed), shred the meat in the pot and stir it into the fat and juices at the bottom, where all the flavor is hanging out. Stuff into steamed buns and serve with pickles, sriracha, sauce, and scallions.

WHOLE WHEAT STEAMED BUNS (MANTOU)

Makes 12 buns

½ cup (120 g) warm water

2¼ teaspoons (8 g or 1 packet) active dry yeast

¼ cup plus 1 teaspoon (54 g) sugar

1½ cups (180 g) bread flour or all-purpose flour

1½ cups (172 g) whole wheat flour

1 teaspoon (3 g) kosher salt

½ teaspoon (2 g) baking powder

½ cup (120 g) whole milk

¼ cup (55 g) rendered pork fat or unsalted butter, at room temperature

Combine the water, yeast, and 1 teaspoon (4 g) of the sugar in the bowl of a stand mixer fitted with the dough hook. Stir and let sit until it gets foamy on top, about 5 minutes.

Add the remaining ¼ cup (50 g) sugar, the flours, salt, and baking powder to the bowl and mix on the lowest setting to combine. Add the milk and pork fat, turn the mixer up a notch, and knead for 10 minutes, or until the dough gathers into a smooth and pliable ball on the hook. Transfer the dough to a lightly oiled bowl and turn it over to coat with the oil. Cover with plastic wrap or a damp kitchen towel and let the dough rise, preferably somewhere warm, until roughly doubled in size, 1½ to 2 hours.

While the dough rises, cut out 12 squares of parchment paper, roughly 3 inches across.

Once the dough has risen, punch it down to deflate and transfer it to a clean work surface. Use a dough cutter or sharp knife to cut the dough into 3 roughly equal pieces. Roll each piece into a log and divide it into 4, giving you 12 dough lumps. One at a time, use one hand to roll each lump into a ball.

Flatten the bottom of each ball slightly by pressing down into your work surface as you roll. Place each ball onto a square of parchment, cover lightly with plastic wrap, and let rise for 40 minutes more.

Pour water to come 3 inches up the sides of a large pot and set up a steamer. Bring to a boil over high heat, then, working in batches if necessary, carefully place the buns inside with some space in between. Steam for 15 minutes, or until the buns are fluffy and dry. Let cool a little (they come out very hot), then slice in half to stuff with deliciousness. They're excellent at room temperature, or they can be refrigerated or frozen in an airtight container. To reheat from frozen, steam until soft (about 10 minutes, but this can vary greatly depending on your steamer setup). If they're refrigerated, microwave for 30 seconds for a pillowy soft, lava-hot bun. Or try the untraditional-yet-undeniably-tasty method—slice in half, brush with butter, and toast or griddle until golden brown.

FROM THE OCEAN

I think it's fair to say we're a New England family. Our grandfather—our mom's dad—was born in Hunan, China, but he lived most of his life near Boston and loved the city enough to have a Red Sox shout-out on his gravestone. Our mother, a lifelong Massachusetts resident, is equally vehement about her allegiance to New England sports teams and her appreciation for seafood. We have her to thank for our love of good fish and seafood, even though she has a shellfish allergy. Dad didn't cook much because of his demanding job in cancer research, but he did teach us how to thread a worm on a hook and catch our own fish. And he was a pro at ordering and appreciating seafood, whether selecting the prime specimen from a fish tank in a Chinese restaurant or tying on a plastic bib and cheerfully demonstrating how to break down a lobster.

obsters are one of the few animals that many of us will kill and cook ourselves in our lifetime. Our mother buys lobsters every time we have out-of-town visitors. She delights in preparing them in the classic New England style—steamed whole, with melted butter—for guests, even though she can't eat them herself. When we were kids, she was always the one to haul the speckled enamel lobster pot out of the pantry and matter-of-factly grab the lobsters, us kids squealing as we watched their insectile legs wave in the air. From her, we learned a love for entertaining and feeding others, combined with a bold, take-no-prisoners approach to what might make others squeamish. But Dad was the one who taught us to value every part of the animal, to do justice to a creature that gave its life for our pleasure. He showed us how to twist the lobster's legs off, one by one, and how to pull the meat up using our teeth. He'd delicately remove the small tail fins to find the miniscule morsel of meat within each tiny pocket, then crack open the body to locate the rib meat and tomalley. It felt like you were winning the game when you managed to extract every magnificent bit of lobster from its shell. I think of him whenever I make Ginger Scallion Lobster Rolls (page 185). More than a recipe, it's a process—almost a ritual—killing an animal, taking its meat, and dressing it in our favorite flavors for our enjoyment and appreciation.

If you don't eat lobster, fish might be the closest you get to cooking a whole animal. It's certainly simpler and more sanitized when you buy fish fillets, and it makes for easy preparation and eating. But roasting or pan-searing a whole fish can be so rewarding. There is a satisfaction in picking through the bones to unearth the best bits of flesh and offering them to your loved ones. Cook the Roasted Whole Fish (page 203) for a dinner party, and eating it together—from head to tail fin—becomes a whole new experience. Then on days when you don't have as much time but still want something special, try the simpler Red-Cooked Fish (page 196).

Another theme to this chapter is a full appreciation of the bounty that comes from the sea. Loving seafood means also respecting that many fish populations are in decline and that we, as thoughtful consumers, should be mindful of the fish we buy. We work with sustainable fisheries, buy fish approved by organizations such as Seafood Watch, and choose sustainable options such as clams and mussels. I'm always amazed that these inexpensive and easy-to-cook ocean proteins are often overlooked. We've paired them with funky, fermented Asian ingredients to highlight their briny flavors, from miso in Miso Butter Mussels (page 195) to fermented black beans in Clams with Black and White Beans over Noodles (page 189). If you're more of a fish person, try experimenting with Broiled Salmon Collars (page 201), the cut favored by so many chefs and fishermen and women.

We've also included our versions of two Chinese restaurant favorites, Salt and Pepper Shrimp (page 180) and Honey Walnut Shrimp (page 183). With additional vegetables and a bright and gingery broccoli salad, these updated takes on the classics are newly appealing while still satisfying those restaurant cravings. Keep it simple and get peeled and prepped shrimp, or go Chinese-style and include the heads and shells. We promise they make for good eating! All in all, we hope you'll use this chapter and its various cooking techniques to enjoy the food of the ocean—claws, fins, bones, shells, and all.

SALT AND PEPPER SHRIMP
WITH SUMMER VEGETABLES

—— GF, DF ——

This is one of our favorite Chinese restaurant dishes—so crunchy, garlicky, and spicy that you eat all the shrimp and then eat the leftover fried bits because they taste so good. Is that just me? We've added colorful slices of corn and peppers, making it kind of a crispy fried Chinese version of a seafood boil.

NOTE: If you can, use sustainably farmed or wild-caught U.S. shrimp. If not buying domestic, do your best to find a certified sustainable source, as imported shrimp can come with social and environmental issues. While we're preaching about shrimp, we'll try to win you over on another topic: eating the shells. We sometimes keep big tubs of fried, seasoned shells around the restaurant for snacking, like shrimpy pink potato chips. With legs. If you're considering shell-on, try smaller shrimp (i.e., 31 to 40 a pound) as the shells tend to be thinner and easier to eat. Serve solo or with Soy Aioli (page 23), or extra Toasted Salt and Peppercorns.

SPECIAL EQUIPMENT: thermometer, spider or slotted spoon, and Dutch oven or large pot for frying

Serves 2 to 4, with sides

1 pound (450 g) shrimp, shell-on or peeled, deveined	2 tablespoons Toasted Salt and Peppercorns (page 20)	1 red bell pepper, seeds removed and sliced crosswise into rings	2 scallions, thinly sliced
1 tablespoon (15 g) Shaoxing wine	Neutral oil, such as canola, for frying	1 jalapeño chile, sliced crosswise into rings	
½ teaspoon (2 g) kosher salt	2 ears of corn, shucked and cut or broken in half	3 cloves garlic, minced	
3 tablespoons (20 g) cornstarch		One 2-inch piece fresh ginger, minced	

Rinse the shrimp, put them in a bowl, and add the wine and salt. Let sit for 20 minutes, then pat dry with paper towels. Wipe out the bowl with a paper towel, put the shrimp back in, and toss with the cornstarch and 1 tablespoon of the toasted salt and peppercorns.

Fill your pot with several inches of oil—1 to 2 quarts should be enough, depending on the size of your pot. Heat over high heat to 375°F (190°C). Line 2 plates with paper towels.

Carefully lift a few pieces of shrimp, shake off the excess cornstarch, and drop them into the oil. Continue until half the shrimp, or as many as can easily fit into the pot, are cooking. Fry for 2 to 3 minutes, until the shrimp are pink with a light golden crust. Using a spider or tongs, transfer to one of the prepared plates. Repeat with the second batch of shrimp.

Let the oil come back up to temperature, then add the corn to the pot. Fry for 2 to 3 minutes, then remove to the second prepared plate. Turn the heat off and carefully move the pot to the back of your stovetop to cool.

(Continued)

Place a wok or large skillet on the front of your stove and turn the heat to medium-high. Using a metal spoon, carefully transfer a few spoonfuls of frying oil to the skillet. Put the bell pepper, chile, garlic, ginger, and scallions into the pan and cook until lightly browned, about 2 minutes. Add the remaining 1 tablespoon toasted salt and peppercorns and stir to combine. Add the shrimp to the skillet with the corn. Toss everything together for 1 to 2 minutes to reheat the shrimp, then transfer to a large serving platter.

Serve immediately, on its own or with your choice of accompaniments.

HONEY WALNUT SHRIMP
WITH GINGER BROCCOLI SALAD

Our take on a popular Chinese restaurant dish, these sweet and crunchy shrimp are beloved by everyone in the family, grandkids included. Paired with a fresh ginger broccoli salad, this dish is impressive enough for dinner parties and also quick enough for a weeknight meal. Get fancy and make your own honey walnut mayonnaise, or just swirl together ingredients you probably already have in your kitchen. Warning: You may find it difficult getting these walnuts to last long enough to make the finished dish. Consider doubling the recipe—extras can be eaten with yogurt at breakfast, salad at dinner, or straight from the jar anytime.

SPECIAL EQUIPMENT: thermometer, spider or slotted spoon, and Dutch oven or large pot for frying

Serves 4

1 cup (120 g) walnut halves

¼ cup (50 g) sugar

1 tablespoon (½ ounce/14 g) unsalted butter

¼ cup (52 g) Honey Walnut Mayonnaise (page 21), or 2 tablespoons (40 g) honey mixed with 3 tablespoons (45 g) mayonnaise

Neutral oil, such as peanut, for frying

1 pound (450 g) medium shrimp, peeled and deveined

Kosher salt

1 large egg, beaten

½ cup (60 g) cornstarch

Fresh cilantro leaves, for garnish (optional)

Ginger Broccoli Salad (recipe follows)

Combine the walnuts, sugar, and butter in a medium nonstick skillet and turn the heat to medium. Stir occasionally at the beginning, then more frequently as the sugar starts to melt. Once the walnuts are fully coated, about 5 minutes, transfer the walnuts to a piece of parchment paper, separate, and let dry.

Place the mayonnaise into a large serving bowl and set aside.

Line a plate with paper towels. Pour oil to come 1 inch up the sides of your pot and heat on medium. Rinse the shrimp and pat dry with paper towels, then lightly season with salt. While the oil heats, set up an assembly line with two shallow bowls, one with the beaten egg and the other with cornstarch, and a large plate. Drop a few shrimp into the egg mixture, then one by one, dredge in the cornstarch and place on the plate. Repeat with the remaining shrimp.

Once the oil reaches 375°F (190°C), add the shrimp in batches of 6 to 8 at a time and separate with tongs or a spider so they don't stick together. Fry until the batter is a dark blond and the exterior is crispy, about 2 minutes. Remove to the prepared plate, then repeat with the remaining shrimp.

Once the shrimp is cooked, add to the bowl with the mayonnaise mixture and toss until the shrimp is thoroughly coated. Top with walnuts and cilantro, if using, and serve immediately, with ginger broccoli salad.

(Continued)

GINGER BROCCOLI SALAD

Kosher salt

2 small heads broccoli
(about 1½ pounds/
680 g)

One 1-inch piece fresh
ginger, grated

⅓ cup (80 g) olive oil

2 tablespoons (30 g)
rice vinegar

Freshly ground black
pepper

Bring a large pot of water to boil and add a good
pinch of salt. Meanwhile, cut the broccoli into bite-
size florets. Peel the large stem and cut it crosswise
into ¼-inch disks. Once the water boils, drop the
broccoli in and cook for about 3 minutes, until it's
bright green and crunchy. Drain and let cool.

Put the ginger, oil, and vinegar in a medium bowl
and whisk to combine. Add the broccoli and toss to coat
in the dressing. Season with salt and pepper and serve.

GINGER SCALLION LOBSTER ROLLS

Ginger scallion lobster from a Cantonese restaurant—cut into shell-on chunks, deep-fried, and tossed with aromatics to be greedily torn apart at the table, elbow to elbow with your siblings and cousins. New England lobster rolls—to be consumed sitting on the weathered gray boards of a clam shack patio by the beach in Maine or on the Cape, your hair still rough with sea salt and sand wedged between your toes.

These are two of my pick-your-last-meal-on-Earth dishes, so combining them for the spectacular flavors of the Chinese version plus the ease of the lobster roll was, to us, the perfect fit for this cookbook. We're not the first to do a ginger scallion lobster roll; our friends from Eventide Oyster Co. in Portland, Maine, do a fantastic version and the first-rate Chinese cooking blog *Woks of Life* has one too. But does anyone else get almost teary-eyed with the feelings of family, summertime, and freedom that come with Chinese-influenced lobster rolls? Do we love it the most? I think it's possible we might.

NOTE: Keep the lobsters refrigerated until time to cook; you can sedate them slightly by placing in the freezer for the last thirty minutes.

SPECIAL EQUIPMENT: large pot (at least 4 quarts) for which you have a lid, lobster crackers and a pick or small fork, or a sharp chef's knife and kitchen shears for extracting the meat

Makes 2 to 4 rolls, depending on how much you like lobster

Two 1½-pound (680 g) live lobsters	3 tablespoons (1½ ounces/40 g) unsalted butter, melted	1 tablespoon (15 g) rice vinegar	Hot dog buns, brioche rolls, or Whole Wheat Steamed Buns (page 175), for serving
¼ cup (60 g) Ginger Scallion Oil (page 18) with lots of ginger and scallion bits	1 tablespoon (15 g) soy sauce	Kosher salt	

Pour water into your pot to come 2 inches up the sides and add a good pinch of salt. Bring to a rolling boil over high heat. Insert a steamer rack to keep the lobsters out of the water if you have one (it's fine if you don't). Carefully put the two lobsters into the pot belly-side down and quickly place the lid on top. Steam for 9 minutes, then check to see if the shells are bright red. If not, put the lid back on and cook for 2 to 4 more minutes, checking every minute or so.

While the lobsters are cooking, fill your sink or a large bowl with ice and cold water.

Using tongs, remove the lobsters from the pot and place them into the ice bath to stop the cooking.

When the shells have cooled, remove the lobsters one at a time and place them on a cutting board. Stay near the sink with paper towels and a trash bag handy; cracking lobsters can be messy business.

Break down the lobsters by grabbing the main body shell in one hand and the tail in the other and twisting firmly to remove the tail. Then grab each claw at the base where it meets the body and twist to remove the claws. The tail and claws make up the majority of the meat, but don't feel you have to throw the rest out. If you're like our dad, you can eat the green tomalley in the main body. You can pull the gills and legs out of the main cavity to extract the rib

meat, or save the main body for stock. We do what our dad taught us: snack on the lobster legs and fins while breaking down the rest of the body.

Remove the tail meat by cutting the tail in half lengthwise with a chef's knife, cutting open the underside with kitchen shears, or using a fork to carefully pull out the meat. Cut into bite-size pieces and place in a medium bowl.

Remove the claw meat by using a lobster cracker to crack open each claw and each segment beneath. Use a lobster pick, a small fork, or your fingers to extract the meat, cut into bite-size pieces, and add to the bowl with the tail meat. Once all the meat has been extracted, it can be refrigerated overnight in a covered container if not serving right away.

When ready to serve, add the ginger scallion oil, butter, soy sauce, and vinegar. Season with salt and mix thoroughly. If your lobsters were on the smaller side, set aside a bit of the sauce and taste before adding more. If they were on the larger side, add a bit more of everything. Taste for seasoning, then spoon onto your roll of choice and eat immediately and joyfully.

CLAMS WITH BLACK AND WHITE BEANS
OVER NOODLES

——— GFO, DF ———

Visiting Boston's Chinatown as kids, we would invariably ogle the fish tanks stuffed with lobsters and eels, poke at the eyes of enormous whole steamed fish, and debate whether or not to eat clams with black bean sauce. We had a love-hate relationship with this classic clam dish, which was fun to eat but sometimes intensely strong with the fermented black beans. Now, I crave their savory umami punch. Here, we mellow it with mild and creamy white beans and we serve the clams over noodles for a Chinese-inflected spaghetti *alle vongole*, or pasta with clam sauce. We love it with fresh ramen or Shanxi noodles, but you could try rice noodles for a gluten-free option—just make sure your chosen noodle is thick enough so it won't be overwhelmed by the splendid briny sauce.

Serves 4 to 6

3 pounds (1.3 kg) small fresh clams, such as littleneck, cherrystone, or Manila

Kosher salt

¼ cup (40 g) fermented black beans, roughly chopped

4 cloves garlic, thinly sliced

One 1-inch piece fresh ginger, minced

2 scallions, divided into white and light green and dark green parts, thinly sliced

3 tablespoons (45 g) Shaoxing wine

2 tablespoons (30 g) soy sauce, preferably low-sodium (use tamari if gluten-free)

1 tablespoon (15 g) oyster sauce

1 tablespoon (13 g) toasted sesame oil

1 tablespoon (13 g) neutral oil, such as canola

12 ounces (340 g) ramen, wheat, or rice noodles, preferably fresh or frozen

One 15-ounce (425 g) can white beans, such as cannellini or great northern, or 2 cups (300 g) cooked white beans, drained

---

Remove the clams from their packaging and rinse them well, discarding any broken or open clams. If you notice a lot of sand or grit, purge the clams by placing them in a large bowl of water that you've salted like the sea for 30 minutes. Remove the clams and discard the water; if there is a lot of sand in the bottom, repeat as needed.

Soak the fermented black beans in a small bowl of cold water for at least 10 minutes or up to overnight; a longer soak will help remove more salt. Meanwhile, put a large pot of salted water to boil on the stove for the noodles. Drain and rinse the fermented black beans, put them in a medium bowl, and add the garlic, ginger, and white and light green scallions, setting the dark green scallions aside for garnish.

Combine the wine, soy sauce, and oyster sauce in a small bowl to have ready for stir-frying.

Heat the sesame oil and neutral oil in a wok or large skillet over medium heat until shimmering. Add the fermented black bean mixture and cook until fragrant and slightly softened, about 2 minutes. Add the clams and stir to combine, then add the wine mixture. Cover, turn the heat to high, and let the clams steam for 4 minutes. Check on the clams and use tongs to transfer any opened clams to a large heatproof bowl. Replace the cover and let any remaining clams steam open, checking every minute or so and transferring open clams to the bowl until they've been cooking about 7 minutes total. Tap any uncooperative clams with your tongs to see if they open; if not, discard them. Turn off the heat, leaving the pan on the stove, and turn up the heat on the pot of water if necessary.

Cook the noodles until slightly undercooked (about a minute less than the package directions). As the noodles cook, remove the clam meat from the shells and discard the shells. We usually leave about a third of the clams in the shell because it looks nice in the bowl. Drain the noodles, reserving 1 cup of the cooking water. Add the noodles and white beans to the clam pan and finish cooking the noodles in the briny, salty sauce, adding a few tablespoons of pasta water if more liquid is needed. Return the clams to the wok and stir for a minute to reheat. Taste the sauce; the black beans, sauce ingredients, and clam brine are all salty, so it's unlikely you'll need additional seasoning. Thin with more pasta water if needed.

Transfer the noodles and clams to a serving bowl and garnish with the reserved scallion greens. Serve immediately.

COCONUT-DASHI CLAM CHOWDER

—— GF, DF ——

As proud New Englanders, we believe clam chowder should always be thick, white, and a little meaty. Our dad loved clam chowder, the platonic ideal being the version served at Legal Sea Foods, provider of chowder to multiple presidential inaugurations and where Andy hooked us up with endless cups over his years working there. While we will always hold true to the look and feel of true clam chowder (nice try, Manhattan clam chowder, but you are just red clam soup), you don't need cups of cream and flour to achieve the rich, viscous consistency of our clam chowder dreams. Instead, we use coconut milk and pureed potatoes to make this version dairy- and gluten-free while kombu (dried kelp) and bonito (dried, smoked, and fermented fish) layer in subtle ocean notes. The final dish manages to honor our childhood chowder memories while highlighting some new favorite ingredients. The main tradition we're willing to step away from: my eight-year-old self would insist on a small plastic packet of dry oyster crackers, but my grown-up self prefers buttered crusty bread.

Serves 4 to 6

COCONUT DASHI

Two 13.5-ounce (400 ml) cans coconut milk

5 strips (18 g) kombu (also known as dried kelp)

One 4-inch piece fresh ginger, sliced in half lengthwise

¼ cup (3 g) bonito flakes (also known as katsuobushi)

CLAMS

1 tablespoon (13 g) olive oil

½ medium onion, sliced

3 cloves garlic, smashed

3 bay leaves

1½ cups (360 g) dry white wine or water

50 (about 2 pounds/900 g) small clams, such as littleneck, rinsed

OTHER INGREDIENTS

3 large Yukon Gold or russet potatoes, cubed

2 tablespoons (25 g) olive oil

6 slices thick-cut bacon, cut into bite-size pieces

½ medium onion, diced

½ cup (110 g) dry white wine

Freshly ground black pepper

MAKE THE COCONUT DASHI

Combine the coconut milk, kombu, ginger, and bonito flakes in a medium saucepan. Bring to a simmer over medium heat, then reduce the heat and cook at a low simmer for about 30 minutes to infuse the coconut milk with all the flavors. You should be able to taste the difference as the lightly sweet and creamy coconut flavor develops savory, briny notes.

STEAM THE CLAMS

While the dashi is cooking, heat the oil with the onion, garlic, bay leaves, and wine in a large pot for which you have a lid over medium heat. Once it comes to a simmer, add the clams, cover, and steam for 10 minutes. Check to see if most of the clams have opened; if not, cover again and steam for another 3 to 5 minutes. Strain, reserving the cooking liquid and clams separately, and let cool, tapping any closed clams and discarding any that don't open in response. Rinse the pot and return to the stove. Once cooled, remove the clams from their shells and set aside with the clam cooking liquid (you should have about 2 cups).

FINISH THE DISH

Once the coconut milk has infused, use tongs to remove the ginger and kombu from the pot and discard. Add the potatoes to the coconut dashi and cook until softened, about 15 minutes, then remove from the heat. If desired, puree about a third of the coconut milk and potatoes in a food processor or blender to thicken the broth (skip for a thinner broth).

Using the pot you steamed the clams in, heat the oil over medium heat until shimmering. Add the bacon and cook until it starts to brown, about 3 minutes. Add the diced onion and cook until softened but not browned, about 6 minutes. Add the clams and wine and let the wine reduce for 2 to 3 minutes, then add the reserved clam cooking liquid. Add the coconut and potato mixture and mix thoroughly.

Bring to a light simmer and taste for seasoning—with the savory kombu, bonito, and bacon, you may not need any salt, but I like lots of black pepper. Serve immediately, with crusty hunks of bread or, for nostalgia's sake, oyster crackers.

MISO BUTTER MUSSELS
WITH BOK CHOY

—— GFO ——

Growing up in Boston, mussels were an easy and affordable seafood option. This recipe takes the white wine and butter from a classic French *moules marinières* and adds in our kitchen essentials of miso and scallions. The miso melts into the butter and the briny mussel juice to make an unexpectedly rich and savory broth. It's one of my favorite weeknight meals, requiring only fifteen-ish minutes from slicing your scallions to sitting at the table with dinner steaming in front of you. Besides being inexpensive and simple to prepare, there's a huge side benefit: Mussels are one of the most sustainable proteins available. Farmed mussels, considered a Best Choice by Seafood Watch, require no feed, as they gather nourishment from surrounding ocean waters and even help clean the water. Wild mussels, available around New England, are a good alternative. Feel free to try different leafy greens in place of the bok choy, but no matter what you choose, make sure to have some good crusty bread or steamed buns on the table.

Serves 4

1 cup (225 g) dry white vermouth, or 1½ cups (340 g) dry white wine

6 tablespoons (3 ounces/85 g) unsalted butter

2 tablespoons (35 g) miso paste, preferably white miso for a subtler flavor

4 scallions, thinly sliced

3 cloves garlic, thinly sliced

1 bay leaf

2 sprigs thyme

About 1 pound (450 g) bok choy, stems and leaves separated and chopped

2 pounds (960) mussels, rinsed and debearded if necessary (i.e., remove the hairy bit attached to the outside)

Fresh parsley, chopped, for serving

Crusty bread, or buttered and toasted Whole Wheat Steamed Buns (page 175), for serving (omit if gluten-free)

Put the vermouth, butter, miso, scallions, garlic, bay leaf, and thyme into a Dutch oven or other pot that will fit the mussels comfortably and for which you have a lid. Turn the heat to medium and let the butter and miso and spices mingle, stirring occasionally, until the mixture starts to bubble lightly. Add the bok choy stems and cook, stirring, for 1 minute. Add the leaves and stir to combine.

Turn the heat up slightly, add the mussels, and cover. Let sit for 3 minutes—this is a good time to pop your bread in the toaster or oven—then uncover and give the mussels a quick stir. Cover and cook for another 2 to 4 minutes, then stir again, coating the mussels with sauce. By now, most of the mussels should have opened. Tap any stubborn mussels with your spoon to see if they open; if not, discard them.

Ladle the mussels and broth into bowls and sprinkle with the parsley. Serve right away, with a crusty baguette or steamed buns.

RED-COOKED FISH

—— GFO, DF ——

Red cooking, or *hong shao,* describes a popular Chinese technique of braising in soy sauce, cooking wine, and aromatics, which results in a sauce so simple yet intoxicating that you may consider drinking it from the bowl. We won't judge, but pouring it over fluffy steamed white rice might get you fewer stares at the dining table. No matter how you eat it, we love how quickly this dish comes together with a good piece of fish and the trinity of Chinese aromatics.

Look for a firm white fish such as bass, barramundi, or tilapia that is sustainably caught or farmed. This recipe calls for two fillets, but if you're not squeamish about fish heads, serving a whole fish of 1 to 1½ pounds makes for a great traditional presentation. Get the fish cleaned and descaled at the fish counter, then cut 3 or 4 diagonal slits across each side of the body before cooking. Serve with sides such as Stir-Fried Greens (page 48) or Ginger Broccoli Salad (page 184) and White Rice (page 14).

Serves 2, with sides

2 firm white fish fillets, about 6 ounces (170 g) each	6 thin slices fresh ginger	½ cup (120 g) Shaoxing wine	2 teaspoons (8 g) sugar
2 tablespoons (26 g) neutral oil, such as canola	3 cloves garlic, sliced	2 tablespoons (30 g) soy sauce (substitute tamari if gluten-free)	Thinly sliced scallions and chopped cilantro, for garnish (optional)
	2 scallions, cut into 2-inch pieces		

Pat the fish dry on both sides with a paper towel and let sit while you prepare the sauce. This dish cooks up quickly, so set up your *mise en place* (translation: slice your aromatics and measure out the wine, soy sauce, and sugar into a small bowl) before starting to cook.

Line a plate with a paper towel. Heat the oil in a wok or heavy-bottomed skillet not too much larger than the fillets over medium-high heat until shimmering. Add the ginger and garlic and cook until they start to brown, about 4 minutes. Using tongs, remove the ginger and garlic and place on the prepared plate. Pick up the fish and carefully place it into the wok skin-side down—try to place it directly in the center of the pan on the first try. This is because as soon as you drop the fish, it will stick to the surface of the pan and refuse to budge. Wherever it falls, leave it for the next few minutes so the skin can crisp up and release itself from the pan. Use a spatula to press the

fish down if it starts to buckle, or carefully swirl the pan so the oil moves around the fish, but do your best to restrain yourself from moving it.

Check after 4 minutes to see if the fish will lift easily. If not, give it another minute; if so, carefully flip it over and cook for 1 minute. (If you're using whole fish, give the second side 5 minutes.) Add the ginger and garlic back to the pan, then toss in the scallions and add the wine, soy sauce, and sugar (keep your hands out of the way, as the liquid will erupt in a puff of steam). Let the fish braise in the liquid, occasionally scooping up some of the liquid with a spoon and pouring over the fish that's not submerged, 3 minutes for thin fillets, a few more for very thick fillets or whole fish.

Using tongs or a spatula, transfer the fillets to a shallow bowl, skin-side up. Pour the sauce over the fish and serve immediately, sprinkled with sliced scallions and chopped cilantro, if using.

FISH WITH FENNEL, CILANTRO, AND SESAME OIL

—— GF, DF ——

Sometimes I'm in the mood for a fast and furious fish dish, like Red-Cooked Fish (page 196) with its seared, passionately crunchy skin that demands your attention at the stovetop. Other times, it's nice to have a fish recipe that takes it easy, one that allows you to chat with your guests and sip a glass of wine as this magical combination of flavors puts in some work—the fennel mellows, the sesame gets all toasty and warm, the almost creamy but dairy-free sauce melts into the fish. We love the results of slow-roasting fish; after cooking the fennel at a slightly higher temperature, you turn the oven temperature down so the fish stays soft and tender, protected by a bed of fennel on the bottom and the bright and herbaceous sauce on top. Leftovers are marvelous piled onto cream cheese–slathered toast or tossed atop a salad or Market Bowl (page 142).

Serves 4 or more, with sides

1 large or 2 small whole fennel bulbs with stalks and fronds

¼ cup (52 g) toasted sesame oil

¼ teaspoon (1 g) kosher salt, plus a pinch

1 medium shallot, finely chopped (about ¼ cup/35 g)

¼ cup (10 g) loosely packed fresh cilantro leaves and stems

One ½-inch piece ginger, minced

1 tablespoon (15 g) rice vinegar

¼ teaspoon (1 g) ground white pepper

1½ pounds (675 g) fish (four 6-ounce/170-g fillets of a relatively firm fish like salmon or barramundi, or one massive piece of fish like wild-caught salmon)

Preheat the oven to 350°F (175°C).

Separate the fennel bulbs from the stalks and leaves. Trim the bottoms of the bulbs and remove any dark spots with a vegetable peeler. Thinly slice the bulbs using a mandoline or sharp chef's knife and set aside ¼ cup of the fronds. The remainder can be added to Local Greens Pesto (page 79) or used in place of dill fronds; we freeze the stalks for the next time we're making stock.

Put the fennel slices in a roasting pan large enough to fit the fish fillets side by side (a little overlap is OK). Drizzle with 2 tablespoons of the oil, sprinkle all over with a pinch of salt, and use your hands to coat the fennel with the oil and salt. Bake for 20 minutes.

Meanwhile, combine the reserved fennel fronds with the shallot and cilantro and finely chop by hand or in a food processor. Add the ginger, vinegar, remaining ¼ teaspoon salt, white pepper, and the remaining 2 tablespoons oil and stir or pulse to combine.

Turn the oven temperature down to 250°F (120°C). Carefully pull the pan out of the oven, lay the fillet(s) on top of the fennel (skin-side down if there is skin), and spread the cilantro-shallot mixture evenly across the top of the fish. Put the pan back in the oven and bake for 15 to 20 minutes, maybe a bit less for very thin fillets or more for thick ones. Eyeball the fish first to see if it has turned opaque. If it has, stick a fork into the thickest section to see if the fish flakes easily; if not, check again in a few minutes.

Serve hot, warm, or at room temperature with rice or grains and vegetables.

BROILED SALMON COLLARS

—— GFO, DF ——

Our less-waste, nose-to-tail, root-to-leaf philosophy extends beyond meat and vegetables whenever possible. At one of our favorite restaurants, Cafe Sushi in Cambridge, Massachusetts, our friend Seizi and his team always send us crispy, glistening fish collars to pick apart while we savor their sushi. As fish experts, they know that some of the richest, most flavorful flesh lies in this "neck" area, behind the head and the gills and extending down the sides to the pectoral fins. The other benefit of this cut is the price—as a piece that people often don't eat, I've found it at one-fifth to one-twentieth of the price of a fillet from the same fish. You might trade ease of eating for the cost savings, but if you'll wrestle to get the best meat off a sparerib, you'll understand the satisfaction of digging into the pocket behind the fins to reach the most succulent salmon you might ever have eaten. We've got three sauce suggestions, all very simple, so the flavor of the fish shines through. Each has only a few ingredients and barely any prep, so you can put the work into extracting every little morsel of deliciousness.

To find fish collars, sometimes labeled as fish necks, visit a local fishmonger or seafood counter that breaks down their own fish. Calling ahead can be a good idea, and consider other options like yellowtail, bass, or lingcod. You can use this technique for oft-discarded cuts like salmon bones or salmon spines. Collars are also great for grilling over high heat.

Serve alongside White Rice (page 14) or Soy Ginger Noodle Salad (page 126). Leftovers of any kind are fantastic tucked into fish tacos or atop a big bowl of Rice Porridge (page 31).

NOTES: Using low-sodium soy sauce will give you more control over the final seasoning levels. Feel free to add in additional herbs and spices.

Serves 4 or more, with sides

2 to 3 pounds (900 to 1.3 kg) salmon or other fish collars

Kosher salt

CITRUS CHILI SAUCE

¼ cup (60 g) chili garlic sauce or sambal oelek

3 tablespoons (40 g) olive oil

2 tablespoons (40 g) honey

1½ tablespoons (22 g) fresh lemon juice (about ½ lemon)

1 tablespoon (15 g) fresh lime juice (about ½ lime)

GARLIC SESAME SAUCE

¼ cup (60 g) soy sauce (substitute tamari if gluten-free)

3 tablespoons (30 g) Chinese sesame paste or tahini

2 tablespoons (26 g) toasted sesame oil

1 tablespoon (15 g) rice vinegar

2 cloves garlic, grated

HONEY SOY GINGER SAUCE

¼ cup (60 g) soy sauce (substitute tamari if gluten-free)

2½ tablespoons (50 g) honey

2 tablespoons (30 g) rice vinegar

2 tablespoons (26 g) olive oil

One 1-inch piece ginger, grated

(Continued)

Turn the broiler on, to high if available, and position an oven rack so the fish will be about 4 inches from the broiler. While it heats up, cover a baking sheet or roasting pan with aluminum foil. Whisk your sauce ingredients of choice together in a small bowl and taste for seasoning. Rinse the collars and pat them dry with paper towels. Sprinkle lightly with salt, brush with sauce, and place skin-side down onto the foil-lined pan.

Place the pan under the broiler, leaving the oven door slightly ajar so you can keep an eye out and turn the pan as needed to make sure it cooks evenly. Once the tops are cooked, 4 to 6 minutes, carefully pull the pan out and use tongs to flip the collars. Brush with the sauce again, put back in the oven, and broil until the skin turns golden brown and delightfully, deliciously crispy, about 5 minutes.

Serve with any remaining sauce for drizzling or dipping, with your side of choice.

ROASTED WHOLE FISH
WITH SUMMER TOMATOES AND THE CHINESE TRINITY

———— GFO, DF ————

Mid-spring of 2010 was a special time for our family: Irene turned twenty years old; our mom celebrated her sixtieth birthday, and our dad marked seventy years. Naturally, we threw a 150th birthday party to mark this momentous occasion. We invited everyone we knew to our parents' backyard and spit-roasted a pig, baked a dozen desserts, and tossed a fifteen-pound bass on the grill. While it's hard to beat the mesmerizing sight of a suckling pig spinning over a fire, the sleeper hit of the event might have been that enormous tender, flaky fish. Reminiscent of the steamed whole fish we'd eat at banquet tables in Chinese restaurants but with a crispy, crackly, flame-kissed skin, it was the perfect outdoor incarnation of a special-occasion family meal.

This fish is a scaled-down version of that magnificent creature, sized for a dinner party rather than a once-in-a-family-lifetime backyard bash. It's inspired by the traditional Cantonese steamed fish, which is strewn with thinly sliced ginger and scallions before a sizzling soy sauce is poured on top. We add cherry tomatoes for a sweet summery touch and roast it in the oven so you can cook a much larger fish. If, like us, you get nervous about cooking an expensive fish and go in and test it repeatedly, don't worry: all evidence will be buried by the colorful cascade of tomatoes and aromatics. It may not be sized for a 150th birthday, but it makes a seriously impressive statement at the dinner table.

Serve with sides such as Stir-Fried Greens (page 48), Ginger Broccoli Salad (page 184), or Roasted Miso Maple Potatoes (page 107) and lots of White Rice (page 14) to soak up the sauce. Leftover fish is excellent on top of Rice Porridge (page 31) or in fish tacos with Cabbage Pickles (page 25), sour cream and salsa.

NOTE: You want a whole head-on fish that has been cleaned, scaled, and gutted. Most fish markets and even supermarkets will do this for you. If you're having trouble finding larger fish, try calling ahead to a local fishmonger and putting in a special order. You'll also need a large serving platter, deep enough to hold a good pour of sauce.

Serves 4 to 8, with sides

One 4- to 5-pound (1.75 to 2.25 kg) whole fish, such as bass, salmon, snapper, or arctic char

Kosher salt

1 cup (240 g) Shaoxing wine

½ cup (120 g) soy sauce (substitute tamari if gluten-free)

⅓ cup (105 g) honey

½ cup (105 g) toasted sesame oil

1 pint cherry or grape tomatoes, halved, or 2 cups (300 g) diced tomatoes

3 scallions, thinly sliced

2 cloves garlic, thinly sliced

One 2-inch piece ginger, thinly julienned

Fresh cilantro leaves, for garnish (optional)

(Continued)

Preheat the oven to 400°F (205°C). Lightly salt the fish inside and out; it doesn't need too much seasoning, as the sauce will be quite salty.

Put the fish in a baking dish or roasting pan or on a baking sheet. If you're planning to serve it in a different vessel, place it on a lightly oiled sheet of aluminum foil so you can transfer it easily. Roast for 5 to 8 minutes per pound, or possibly more (cook times can vary considerably depending on your oven and the thickness of the fish).

While the fish is in the oven, combine the wine, soy sauce, and honey in a medium saucepan over medium-high heat. Bring to a boil, then continue to boil until reduced by half, to the consistency of flat cola, 10 to 15 minutes. Turn the heat off and let sit until the fish is done.

Once you've reached the 5 minutes per pound mark, use a small, sharp knife to poke the fish at its thickest point and lift it slightly to look at the flesh. It should be flaky and opaque and lift easily from the backbone. If it's translucent, gooey, or sticking to the bone, cook for another minute per pound and test

again, repeating as necessary. Carefully remove the fish from the oven and let rest while you make the sauce.

While the fish is resting, add the oil, tomatoes, scallions, garlic, and ginger to the saucepan with the soy sauce mixture and turn the heat back to medium-high. Heat until the sauce begins to sizzle and simmer. If you're transferring the fish to a serving platter, make sure it's heatproof and deep enough to hold a good amount of sauce. When you're ready to serve, spoon the tomatoes on top of the fish, sprinkle with cilantro, if using, then pour the sauce over the whole fish and platter. (Any extra sauce can be tossed with noodles for an easy snack.)

To serve, push aside the top layer of skin and eat or discard it, then lift the flesh from the top of the fish. Divide among plates, making sure to spoon some sauce and tomatoes onto each serving. Once the top of the fish has been picked clean, lift the backbone and discard it to get to the rest of the meat, or flip the fish over to take care of the other side. Don't forget to eat the fish cheeks!

CH. 8

DRINKS AND DESSERTS

Our dad would always say "Eat dessert first!" with a cheeky grin on his face. I don't remember him doing it too often, but I appreciate the sentiment behind the statement. Since he passed away a few years ago, I can't talk to him more about his dessert philosophy, but I'm guessing he meant that we should prioritize the sweet things in life. Enjoy the simple pleasures.

Dad's idea of dessert was slowly carving a whole papaya into juicy pieces at the kitchen table. He preferred simple and natural when it came to sweets. While we'll never turn down a decadent cake or an extravagant pastry, we tend to follow his lead when making dessert at home, embracing lots of fruits and even vegetables. Carrots, beets, and squash might not be the first ingredients that come to mind when you think of dessert, but we love their earthy sweetness, not to mention rich colors and nutritional benefits. Whether their jewel tones shine brightly like in our Honey Beet Blondies (page 217), or hide in plain sight as in Carrot Chocolate Mousse (page 213), our dinner guests can rarely tell there are root vegetables among the ingredients. There's an intriguing complexity to the sweetness rather than a straight shot of sugar.

We also appreciate dessert recipes without dozens of steps, dishes that take advantage of time over effort. We don't have a pastry chef at our restaurant, so desserts need to be prepared in advance and easily executed. They translate perfectly for effortless entertaining at home. Corn Graham Cheesecake (page 222) and Oolong Panna Cotta (page 219) can be prepared the morning of or the day before, then they chill in the fridge while you prepare other courses, hang with your guests, or just chill yourself. Some dessert components require a bit more effort: Bourbon butternut custard from the Cranberry Upside-Down Cake (page 214) appeals for some attention at the stove, but can be tended with a glass of wine in hand. The buttery, crisp topping on the Oat Crunch Chocolate Pudding (page 225) demands a few extra steps, but can be saved to adorn other desserts or even breakfast. Try the custard over macerated strawberries (page 220) or the oat crunch on the panna cotta—just as we keep prepped dessert toppings at the restaurant for last-minute garnishes, you can do so at home for easier dessert making.

Also included in this chapter are some enduringly popular drinks from our food truck and restaurant.

They're beloved by our guests because they're distinctive as well as delicious and appreciated by our staff because they're so simple to prepare. With only a few ingredients (sometimes only two!), you can create compelling nonalcoholic drinks for any season. We have limited space and time for drinks in our food truck—you can't make every beverage to order when you're pounding through two hundred orders in a lunch rush—so we prepare syrups in advance, like Haymaker's Punch (page 209) in the summer and Hot Buttered Fire Cider (page 210) in the winter. Then you just add water or apple cider (and perhaps a splash of booze) for an instant party drink: Enjoy the refreshing, vinegary kick of punch at a summer picnic or the spicy notes of fire cider at a holiday dinner.

Whether you choose to eat dessert first or last, we hope you enjoy these sweets and drinks. I love the idea of eating dessert first, and I'll think of my dad every time I do so. But I still tell my daughter, Kira, that she needs to finish her green beans before she can have her chocolate mousse. And then she can have as much as she wants . . . after all, it's full of carrots!

HAYMAKER'S PUNCH

—— V, GF, DF ——

We owe this drink to Caden, one of the longest-standing members of the Mei Mei team and now our senior manager in charge of pretty much everything, including our beverage program. Lightly sweet, with an invigorating acidity, this punch was an instant hit on the food truck. I keep double batches in my fridge to mix with water whenever I want something refreshing (and, according to some people, very healthy).

Serves 4

½ cup (160 g) honey

½ cup (120 g) apple cider vinegar

Several dashes of fruit bitters (we like peach or orange)

In a pitcher or large jar, whisk or shake all the ingredients to combine. Add 5 cups water and whisk or shake again. Serve over ice, possibly with a splash of Prosecco.

WOODSMAN'S REFRESHER

—— V, GF ——

One of Irene's purest memories from her high school semester in Vermont is trudging through snowy woods, freezing and sweating, to explore the sugar bush. She'd dump her pack on the ground and survey the trees, dotted with buckets collecting maple sap as it defrosted inside the trunks. It turns out this lovely liquid is boiled down to a tiny fraction—2 percent—of its initial volume to make one of Vermont's most highly prized products: pure maple syrup. This gorgeous, dark, heavenly stuff was so precious that she'd fill an empty jar or bottle with milk, shake it up, and drink the "woodsman's refresher" to make sure she cleaned out every last drop of the syrup from the bottle. It has become a huge hit on the food truck, and barely requires a recipe, but here it is nonetheless. And while we're on non-recipes, next time it snows, go grab a few cups of snow and mix with a drizzle of maple syrup to make snow cream. You can thank us next winter.

Serves 2

2 cups (480 g) whole milk

2 tablespoons (40 g) dark robust maple syrup

In a jar, shake the milk with the maple syrup to combine and serve immediately over ice.

HOT BUTTERED FIRE CIDER

—— V, GF ——

Here we blend hot mulled cider and the folk remedy known as fire cider, a tonic meant to clear your sinuses, ward off colds, and more. We leave out savory elements like horseradish and garlic present in some traditional fire ciders, but it's still a multi-heat experience with spicy chilies and piquant ginger balanced with honey for sweetness. Then there's a pat of butter as icing on the cake. It sounds a bit weird, we know, but try it and we think you'll be hooked. (Also pictured: Whole Wheat Black Sesame Shortbread, page 226 and Honey Beet Blondies, page 217.)

Serves 6

½ cup (100 g) sliced fresh ginger

One dried hot chile, such as Japones

2 cups (480 g) water

⅓ cup (105 g) honey

⅓ cup (80 g) apple cider vinegar, plus more as needed

4 cups (960 g) apple cider

Salted butter, for serving

Bourbon or dark spiced rum, for serving (optional)

Combine the ginger, chile, and water in a small saucepan. Bring to a simmer over medium heat, then lower the heat, cover, and simmer for 30 to 40 minutes. Strain the liquid into a heatproof container and add the honey and vinegar. Stir to dissolve the honey, then add the apple cider. Taste and add more cider, if desired. Serve hot, with a small pat of butter stirred into each mug and, just maybe, a good glug of bourbon or dark spiced rum.

. CARROT CHOCOLATE MOUSSE .

—— V, GF ——

When invited to make a special farm lunch for our friends at The Food Project using their locally grown vegetables, we knew exactly what to cook for the main courses. But what to do for dessert? We went for chocolate mousse, sweetened with . . . carrots? Turns out you can transform a root vegetable into a smooth and silky chocolate mousse with surprisingly little effort. Chocolate mousse comes in many guises, but we fell for the simplicity of Elizabeth David's recipe from *French Provincial Cooking*. Compared to some versions that favor the yolks or the whites, this uses the whole egg for both richness and lightness (and saves you from wasting food or eating lots of egg white omelets). It's creamy, cool, and, unsurprisingly, our new favorite way to eat carrots.

NOTE: We prefer dark chocolate, about 70 percent cocoa; for a sweeter mousse, use semisweet chocolate, or add 2 teaspoons sugar right before you finish whipping the egg whites.

Serves 4

3 medium carrots, cut into chunks	4 ounces (115 g) dark chocolate, chopped	2 tablespoons (30 g) whole milk	4 large eggs

Set up a steamer with a few inches of water and bring the water to a boil over high heat. Add the carrots and steam until they can easily be pierced by a fork, about 10 minutes. Transfer the carrots to a blender and let cool slightly.

Turn the water down so it's at a low simmer and place a medium to large heatproof bowl on top of the steamer. Add the chocolate and stir until melted. Meanwhile, add the milk to the blender with the carrots and blend until smooth. Add to the melted chocolate and stir until the mixture is uniform, then remove from the heat.

Separate the eggs into yolks and whites (I like to crack the eggs into a small bowl, one at a time, and gently scoop up the yolk with my fingers, letting the white drop through my fingers). Add the yolks to the chocolate mixture, which should still be a bit warm, and whisk to combine.

Put the egg whites into the bowl of a stand mixer fitted with the whisk attachment and beat until they hold soft peaks. Scoop one-third of the egg whites into the chocolate mixture and whisk to combine. Then take the rest of the egg whites and gently pour them into the chocolate mixture. Using a rubber spatula, fold the two together by carefully scooping up the chocolate from the bottom of the bowl and overturning it into the egg whites. The idea is to maintain the puffiness of the aerated egg whites without deflating, so you have a lightly textured mousse rather than a dense chocolate pudding. Work delicately but thoroughly, continuing to fold until the mousse is a uniform pale glossy brown.

Gently transfer the mousse into a serving bowl or small cups and refrigerate until set, at least 1 hour. Serve with whipped cream (page 220), Oat Crunch (page 225), or just by itself.

CRANBERRY UPSIDE-DOWN CAKE
WITH BOURBON BUTTERNUT CUSTARD

——— v ———

Throughout my three years of living in London, I was delighted every time I got a jug of proper custard to pour over my pudding, which is what they often call dessert in England. Back at the restaurant, we call that same sweet sauce *crème anglaise*. Whatever you choose to call this eggy, creamy, pourable liquid, it's magical, like a warm soupy ice cream embrace. We spike it with bourbon to cut through the richness and fold in some butternut squash puree for a unique nutty sweetness. It is therefore not actually proper custard, but we like it all the same.

Spooned over this colorfully dotted upside-down cake, it's sure to impress, but for a simpler presentation, you can serve it over fresh fruit or macerated strawberries (page 220). Given our love for local ingredients, it's no surprise we top this cake with Cape Cod cranberries; they provide a sharp tartness that keeps the dish from being overly sweet. Adapted from a wonderful *Smitten Kitchen* recipe, we've added maple syrup for more New England love, plus a hit of Chinese five-spice, and you've got all we ever want in a pudding. Er . . . dessert.

Serves 6 to 8

CAKE

⅓ cup (105 g) maple syrup

2 cups (8 ounces/ 250 g) fresh or frozen cranberries

3 large eggs

1 cup (227 g) sour cream or plain whole Greek yogurt

8 tablespoons (4 ounces/113 g) unsalted butter, melted and cooled

1 teaspoon (5 g) vanilla extract

2 cups (240 g) all-purpose flour

1 cup (160 g) loosely packed brown sugar

2 teaspoons (8 g) baking powder

½ teaspoon (2 g) five-spice powder

½ teaspoon (2 g) kosher salt

CUSTARD

1½ cups (360 g) heavy cream, or whole milk, or a combination, depending on how rich you want your custard

3 large egg yolks (save the whites for an omelet)

½ cup (80 g) loosely packed brown sugar

1 tablespoon (15 g) bourbon

1 teaspoon (3 g) corn flour (optional; helps stabilize the custard)

1 cup pureed butternut squash (see page xx [[ms 96]] for roasting instructions; omit olive oil and salt)

MAKE THE CAKE

Preheat the oven to 375°F (190°C) and grease a 9-inch round cake pan. Pour the maple syrup into the pan and add the cranberries, pressing the berries into an even layer across the bottom and around the edges.

Combine the eggs and sour cream in a large bowl or the bowl of a stand mixer fitted with the whisk attachment. Whisk, then add the melted butter and vanilla extract and whisk again until smooth. Whisk together the flour, brown sugar, baking powder, five-spice powder, and salt in a medium bowl. Slowly add the flour mixture to the egg mixture and stir, scraping down the bowl, until well combined.

Pour the batter on top of the cranberries and smooth the top with a rubber spatula. Put the cake in the oven and bake for 40 to 50 minutes, until a

fork or cake tester inserted into the center of the cake comes out clean. If the batter is close to overflowing the pan, line a baking sheet with parchment paper and place it on the rack below the cake to catch any spills. Let cool completely, then place a larger plate upside-down over the cake pan and invert to turn the cake out onto the plate.

MAKE THE CUSTARD

Heat the cream in a medium saucepan over low heat, stirring occasionally, until bubbles start to form around the edges of the pan. While you heat the cream, whisk together the egg yolks, brown sugar, bourbon, and corn flour, if using, in a medium bowl.

Carefully pour half of the bubbling cream into the egg mixture, whisking constantly until thoroughly combined, then pour it back into the pot and whisk to incorporate the rest of the cream. Whisk in the butternut squash until thoroughly combined.

Stir the custard with a wooden spoon as it reheats and starts to thicken. Turn off the heat once it starts to simmer and has the texture of melted ice cream. Serve right away, or pour the custard into a bowl and cover the surface with plastic wrap to prevent a skin from forming. To reheat, place the bowl over a pan of lightly simmering water.

To serve, cut generous wedges of the cake and let guests gleefully pour the custard on top.

HONEY BEET BLONDIES

—— v ——

We love blondies, but not when they taste like the whole candy aisle has been chucked in the mix. This version, with an imposing burgundy swirl of roasted beets, manages to be both eye-catching as well as impressively adult- and kid-friendly. Lest you worry that the final product will be too much like a vegetable and not enough like a dessert, none of our taste testers identified the secret root ingredient, even after consuming many, many blondies. Serve these blondies on their own or with ice cream, whipped cream (page 220), or the sauce of your choice. (As pictured on page 211.)

NOTE: To cook the beets, wrap them in foil and roast at 450°F (230°C) for 45 minutes, or steam for about 20 minutes.

Serves 6 to 8

1½ teaspoons (6 g) neutral oil, such as canola, plus more for greasing

1 large beet or 2 small beets, cooked and sliced

1 tablespoon (20 g) honey

8 tablespoons (4 ounces/113 g) unsalted butter, melted and cooled

¾ cup (150 g) tightly packed brown sugar

1 large egg

1 teaspoon (5 g) vanilla extract

1 cup (120 g) all-purpose flour

¼ teaspoon (1 g) kosher salt

Preheat the oven to 350°F (175°C). Grease an 8 x 8-inch baking dish.

Put the beets, honey, and oil into a blender or food processor and blend into a smooth paste. Combine the melted butter and brown sugar in a medium bowl and mix thoroughly. Add the egg and vanilla and stir until smooth. Add the flour and salt and mix until you have a thick, uniform batter.

Pour the pureed beets into the blondie mixture and use a spoon or spatula to swirl the two together.

You're not looking to mix them entirely, but to have ribbons of magenta beet running through chunks of blondie.

Using the spoon or spatula, scrape the mixture into the prepared baking dish and place in the oven. Bake for 25 minutes, or until a fork inserted into the center comes out clean. The blondies are best a bit gooey, so check a few minutes before to avoid overcooking; they'll set a bit more as they cool. Serve, with the accompaniment of your choice, if desired.

OOLONG PANNA COTTA

—— GF ——

As you make this dessert, lean over the pot and inhale deeply as the oolong tea leaves infuse the warm milk. Every time I do this, I'm transported by the unmistakable fragrance to one of my happy places: a big, bustling Chinese banquet restaurant. Steeped into this panna cotta, the tea adds a lovely floral note to an uncomplicated yet elegant dessert that delights all ages. At the restaurant, we pour the mixture into tiny mason jars; without the unmolding of a traditional panna cotta, they're easier to make, simpler to serve, and instantly presentation-worthy. We like to serve ours with something crunchy on top—try Oat Crunch (page 225), crumbled Whole Wheat Black Sesame Shortbread (page 226), or the toasted nuts or cookie crumbles of your choice.

NOTE: We've done lots of variations on this simple dessert in the restaurant. Try jasmine or green tea instead of oolong, or omit the tea bags and whisk in maple syrup to taste.

Serves 4 to 8

3 tablespoons (45 g) cold water	⅓ cup (67 g) sugar	Pinch of kosher salt	2 cups (454 g) plain whole Greek yogurt
2½ teaspoons (7 g) gelatin (usually 1 packet)	1½ cups (360 g) whole milk	5 oolong tea bags, or 1½ tablespoons (10 g) oolong tea leaves	

Put the water and gelatin in a small bowl and stir. Set aside while the gelatin softens, about 10 minutes.

Combine the sugar, milk, and salt in a small saucepan, add the tea, and put over medium-low heat. Cook, stirring occasionally, until the sugar and salt dissolve and the tea has turned the milk a pale chestnut color, about 10 minutes. Don't let the mixture boil. Turn off the heat, then drain or remove the tea bags and discard.

Whisk in the gelatin mixture until smooth and uniform, then whisk in the yogurt. Pour into small containers, then chill in the refrigerator for at least 2 hours, then serve, with your choice of topping.

STRAWBERRIES AND CREAM

—— V, GFO (with gluten-free cookies) ——

Our dad always loved a bowl of strawberries for dessert. He passed on this love of plain, juicy summer berries to his daughters and grandkids, but sometimes it's fun to toss in some spice, cream, and crunch. Macerating the berries in sugar and an acidic liquid helps soften the berries and bring out bright flavors, especially if the berries aren't at their seasonal peak. Rice vinegar, star anise, and cardamom add subtle Chinese overtones to the sweet syrup that results from the maceration, while sour cream brings a refreshing tang to the whipped cream. We love this with the nutty crumble of Whole Wheat Black Sesame Shortbread and some fresh herbs, but feel free to try other cookies or just eat the berries and cream. Or have a bowl of plain berries; we're cool with that too.

Serves 4 to 6

STRAWBERRIES

¼ cup (40 g) loosely packed brown sugar

2 tablespoons (30 g) rice vinegar

1 quart (600 g) strawberries, hulled and cut into bite-size pieces if large

1 star anise

1 cardamom pod, lightly crushed

WHIPPED CREAM

½ cup (120 g) heavy cream

½ cup (113 g) sour cream

2 tablespoons (15 g) powdered sugar

½ teaspoon (3 g) vanilla extract

TOPPINGS

8 pieces Whole Wheat Black Sesame Shortbread (page 226) or other shortbread or cookie of choice

Fresh herbs such as Thai basil, mint, fennel fronds, or lemon balm, for garnish

MACERATE THE STRAWBERRIES

Mix the brown sugar and vinegar in a medium bowl. Add the strawberries, star anise, and cardamom and stir to coat thoroughly. Let sit for at least 30 minutes on the counter, or as long as overnight covered in the refrigerator, stirring occasionally to coat the strawberries evenly. The longer the berries sit, the stronger the infusion.

MAKE THE WHIPPED CREAM

Put the heavy cream and sour cream into a large bowl or the bowl of a stand mixer fitted with the whisk attachment. Whisk rapidly by hand or on medium speed with the mixer until soft peaks form. Add the powdered sugar and vanilla and whisk again until soft peaks return.

Divide the strawberries into 4 small bowls. Crumble 2 cookies into each bowl and top with a large dollop of the whipped cream. Garnish with a scattering of herbs.

CORN GRAHAM CHEESECAKE
WITH BLUEBERRY COMPOTE

———— v ————

This lovely summer dessert highlights our favorite seasonal flavors of corn and blueberries alongside a tangy, creamy filling. A bonus: The no-bake cheesecake filling keeps you away from the heat while the corn graham crust requires just a few minutes in the oven during the sweltering depths of summer. The crust is from one of our former kitchen managers, Ben Stroud, who started as a regular at the food truck. He'd stop by on his way to his job at a kitchen supply store in downtown Boston bearing delightful homemade gifts like cheesy crackers shaped like bumblebees and lard crackers in pig shapes. He made these rich and nutty corn graham crackers, which we've turned into a crust, but you could always shape them into pigs or bumblebees. Don't forget to drop by and bring us some; we'll be waiting at the food truck!

NOTE: If you're looking for a summer dessert that doesn't require heat at all, you can make the cheesecake on its own, use crumbled store-bought cookies, or swap the compote for fresh fruit or macerated strawberries (page 220).

Serves 6 to 8

CORN GRAHAM CRUST

¼ cup (60 g) whole milk

2 tablespoons (40 g) honey

1 cup (120 g) all-purpose flour

½ cup (100 g) tightly packed brown sugar

½ cup (60 g) corn flour

½ teaspoon (3 g) baking soda

¼ teaspoon (1 g) kosher salt

4 tablespoons (2 ounces/55 g) cold unsalted butter, cubed

CHEESECAKE FILLING

8 ounces (225 g) cream cheese, at room temperature

8 ounces (225 g) mascarpone cheese, at room temperature

One 14-ounce (396 g) can sweetened condensed milk

1½ tablespoons (22 g) fresh lemon juice

1 teaspoon (5 g) vanilla extract

BLUEBERRY COMPOTE

1 pint (about 350 g) blueberries

3 tablespoons (37 g) sugar

3 tablespoons (45 g) water

One ½-inch piece fresh ginger, minced or grated on a Microplane

---

MAKE THE CRUST

Preheat the oven to 350°F (175°C).

Whisk the milk and honey in a small bowl and set aside. Combine the all-purpose flour, brown sugar, corn flour, baking soda, and salt in a large bowl or food processor and stir or pulse to combine. Add the butter cubes and mix with your fingers or pulse with the blade until the mixture resembles coarse crumbs.

Blend in the milk and honey mixture until just combined.

Knead the dough gently to form a sticky ball and place it on a piece of parchment paper on the counter. Place another piece of parchment paper on top to minimize sticking and use a rolling pin to flatten the dough to roughly ½-inch thickness. Discard the top piece of paper and transfer the bottom piece to a baking sheet. Bake for about 8 minutes, until golden brown, then remove from the oven and let cool on the sheet.

Crumble the graham crust into pieces and press into a 9-inch springform pan or sprinkle into small bowls for a free-form cheesecake.

MAKE THE FILLING

Put the cream cheese and mascarpone into a large bowl or the bowl of a stand mixer fitted with the paddle attachment and mix until smooth. Continue to stir while drizzling in the sweetened condensed milk, lemon juice, and vanilla. Once the mixture is smooth and uniform, use a spoon or spatula to spread it on top of the crust. Chill for at least 2 hours, or overnight to get it more sliceable.

MAKE THE COMPOTE

Combine the blueberries, sugar, water, and ginger in a small saucepan. It won't seem like much liquid at first, but the blueberries will release lots of juice as they heat. Bring to a simmer over medium heat and cook, stirring occasionally, until the sauce is thickened, 8 to 10 minutes. Let cool slightly before serving. The compote can be chilled and stored in the refrigerator for up to a week.

Top the chilled cheesecake with the blueberry compote and serve.

OAT CRUNCH CHOCOLATE PUDDING

—— v ——

We put this rich chocolaty dessert topped with toasty buttery oats onto the restaurant menu to show off New England oats. They're from a cool company called Maine Grains that sources sustainable grains and uses a traditional stone milling process to preserve the nutritional content. Irene supported their crowdfunding campaign before we opened the food truck, and we love how they're all about building a vibrant food community. Portion the pudding into small cups or pour it into a pie tin for a shared dessert—either way, it's a joyfully crunchy, creamy way to end a meal.

Serves 4 to 8

PUDDING

¾ cup (150 g) sugar

¼ cup (30 g) cornstarch

2 heaping tablespoons (35 g) unsweetened cocoa powder

¼ teaspoon (1 g) kosher salt

2 cups (480 g) whole milk

½ cup (120 g) heavy cream

8 ounces (225 g) semisweet or bittersweet chocolate chips

1½ teaspoons (8 g) vanilla extract

2 tablespoons (30 g) rum (we like dark but use white in a pinch)

OAT CRUMB

4 tablespoons (2 ounces/55 g) softened salted or unsalted butter

⅓ cup (53 g) loosely packed brown sugar

Kosher salt

1 cup (100 g) rolled oats

Whipped cream (page 220) for serving

MAKE THE PUDDING

Combine the sugar, cornstarch, cocoa powder, and salt in a medium bowl and whisk until well combined. Add 1 cup of the milk and whisk until smooth with no lumps. Pour into a medium saucepan and add the remaining 1 cup milk and the heavy cream. Heat on medium, stirring occasionally, until the mixture thickens, 8 to 10 minutes. Remove from heat and stir in the chocolate chips, vanilla, and rum. Whisk until the mixture is smooth again, pour into serving vessel(s), and refrigerate for at least 2 hours to firm up and chill.

MAKE THE OAT CRUMB

Preheat the oven to 350°F (175°C). Line a baking sheet with parchment paper.

Using a mixer or whisk, beat the butter and brown sugar until fluffy. If using unsalted butter, stir in a good pinch of salt. Add the oats and mix with your hands until the oats are well coated. Spread the oats onto the prepared sheet and bake for 12 to 15 minutes, until golden brown. Let cool.

To serve, top the pudding with generous spoonfuls of oat crumb and whipped cream. Store leftover oat crumb in an airtight container on the counter for up to a week; it will be delicious on top of anything sweet and creamy.

WHOLE WHEAT BLACK SESAME SHORTBREAD

———— v ————

These little cookies remind us of the sesame candy you sometimes find in Asian markets, but with a rounder, richer taste. It's a great showcase for flavorful flour; we use Massachusetts-grown spelt flour from our friends at Four Star Farms. The sweet and savory squares make for a tasty snack on their own, or crumble them over Strawberries and Cream (page 220), Oolong Panna Cotta (page 219), or a plain bowl of ice cream . . . the list goes on. (As pictured on page 211.)

Makes about 24 cookies

1 cup (8 ounces/ 225 g) unsalted butter, softened	½ cup plus 2 tablespoons (125 g) sugar	2 cups (230 g) spelt or whole wheat flour	2 tablespoons (16 g) black sesame seeds
	1½ tablespoons (20 g) toasted sesame oil	¾ teaspoon (2 g) kosher salt	

Put the butter and sugar in the bowl of a stand mixer fitted with the paddle attachment and beat on medium speed until light and fluffy. Add the oil and mix until combined. Scrape down the sides of the bowl, then add the flour and salt. Mix on the lowest speed until incorporated, then raise the speed to medium and mix until the dough just starts to come together and no longer looks dry.

Turn the dough out onto a piece of plastic wrap and form it into a roughly ½-inch-thick rectangle. Wrap the rectangle in plastic wrap and place in freezer for 15 minutes while you preheat the oven to 350°F (175°C).

Take the dough out of the freezer and place on parchment paper or a silicone baking mat. Roll into a uniform ¼-inch-thick sheet, then sprinkle the sesame seeds evenly across the top. Use your fingers or the bottom of a baking sheet to gently press them into the top of the dough.

Using a dough cutter or knife, cut the dough into 1-inch squares and separate them slightly. Slide the parchment or baking mat carefully onto a baking sheet and bake for 20 to 25 minutes, until light golden brown around the edges. Let cool on the sheet, then store in an airtight container for up to 1 week.

MISO SESAME CHOCOLATE CHIP COOKIES

—— v ——

These are my ultimate chocolate chip cookies, containing all the things a cookie should have (dark chocolate and oats for an appealing nubby texture, but not so many oats that this is an oatmeal cookie) and none of the things it shouldn't (raisins, obviously). To take matters further, we use half spelt flour, an ancient wheat variety that provides a richer, more flavorful edge over refined white flour. And then there are our secret weapons: savory miso and sesame paste. Whether people find the flavors familiar or not, most don't pick up on them—they just stuff the cookie in their face. Then they pause to think, marvel at the depth of flavor, note the extra hit of savoriness . . . and ask for another.

Makes about 22 cookies

1½ cups (180 g) all-purpose flour

1½ cups (172 g) spelt or whole wheat flour

1 cup (100 g) old-fashioned rolled oats

2 teaspoons (8 g) baking powder

1 teaspoon (6 g) baking soda

1 teaspoon (3 g) kosher salt

1 cup (8 ounces/225 g) cold salted butter, cut the size of sugar cubes

1 cup (200 g) tightly packed brown sugar

1 cup (200 g) granulated sugar

2 large eggs

1 teaspoon (5 g) vanilla extract

2 tablespoons (35 g) miso paste, preferably white miso for a subtler flavor

2 tablespoons (20 g) Chinese sesame paste or tahini (or omit and increase the miso by 1 tablespoon/20 g)

8 ounces (225 g) dark chocolate chips or chunks (or substitute white chocolate, if you like)

Preheat the oven to 350°F (175°C), with two racks evenly spaced inside. Line 2 baking sheets with parchment paper or silicone baking mats. (The cookies should just fit, but spread out to 3 baking sheets if you want to ensure they don't run into each other.)

Whisk the flours, oats, baking powder, baking soda, and salt in a large bowl. Combine the butter and sugars in the bowl of a stand mixer fitted with the paddle attachment. Mix on low speed until well combined, about 2 minutes. Scrape down the sides of the bowl, then add the eggs and mix on low speed until uniform. Add the vanilla, miso paste, and sesame paste, then the flour mixture, and continue to mix until the dough is barely coming together.

Scrape down the sides of the bowl again and add the chocolate chips, then mix one last time to distribute the chocolate chips throughout the batter.

Use a spoon (we use a 2-ounce disher) to scoop out balls of dough and place them evenly on the baking sheets. I aim for 11 cookies per sheet, with a row of 4 cookies then 3 cookies, then 4 cookies. Bake for 18 to 22 minutes, switching the sheets halfway through, until the cookies have flattened and are light golden brown. I like to pull them when they're cooked through on the bottom but still a bit gooey in the center and eat them warm; if you let them cool and wrap them in an airtight container, they'll last for up to 4 days, or in the freezer for up to a month.

ACKNOWLEDGMENTS

First and foremost, to Mom and Dad—thank you for everything, always. This book is for you.

To Sara, Ivan, and the rest of the Bercholz family—thank you for making this dream come true. Juree, thank you for the long, fun phone calls and for helping to shape a torrent of words into something cohesive. And an enormous thanks to everyone else at Roost for helping to bring this book to life. We love you guys and what you do.

To our agent Lori Galvin—we're so glad the food truck ended up parked near your office! Thanks for the support, the wit, and the wisdom—we're lucky to have you in our corner.

To Michael Piazza, our photographer extraordinaire—thank you for your tireless efforts to make this book spectacularly gorgeous. Working with you has been a master class in food photography and a creative inspiration. And to Robyn Maguire, for being endlessly helpful and just all-around awesome.

To the amazing, incomparable Mei Mei crew—you guys kick ass all the time. And especially to the small council—Emily, Caden, and Peter—for keeping the lights on while we worked on this project (and also every other day).

To everyone who cooked a recipe or read a draft—especially Jessica Bridger and Jessica Coughlin—thank you for being a part of this creation.

To all our farmers, producers, growers, ranchers, fermenters, brewers, winemakers, chefs, food truckers, industry friends, community organizers, educators, and our wonderful guests and regulars—aka the extended Mei Mei family—thank you for the support, love, and delicious ingredients. We couldn't do what we do without you.

And to our families—to grandmas and grandpas, aunts and uncles, cousins, and more, and especially to Leo and Kira, Jackson, and Chris—we love you forever.

RESOURCES

ASIAN PRODUCTS

I've always been lucky enough to live near a location of the Korean supermarket wonderland that is **H Mart**, but if you don't, thankfully there is HMart.com! It's a great online source for Asian pantry items from soy sauce to gochujang to surprise delights like Cheese Hot Chicken Instant Ramen.
www.hmart.com

An organic source for soy sauce, sesame oil, noodles, and other grocery items, in particular Japanese ones, is **Eden Foods**.
www.edenfoods.com

If you don't live near an Asian supermarket or can't find what you like at HMart.com, **Amazon** has everything from Sichuan peppercorns to fermented black beans to our favorite brand of curry paste.
www.amazon.com

GRAINS AND FLOURS, ETC.

Anson Mills specializes in organic heirloom grains; **Bob's Red Mill** is employee-owned and operated and offers an excellent selection of gluten-free and other specialized products.
www.ansonmills.com
www.bobsredmill.com

Our friends at **Four Star Farms** in Northfield, Massachusetts, ship their fantastic spelt, rye berries, and other whole grains.
www.fourstarfarms.com

FARMERS' MARKETS AND FARM PRODUCTS

Whenever I'm in a new city, I look online for a nearby farmers' market to visit. The website **Local Harvest** can help you find a farmers' market as well as farms, CSA (community supported agriculture) programs, and events.
www.localharvest.org

The online marketplace **Farm to People** supports small-batch producers like our favorite biodynamic kimchi makers, Hawthorne Valley Farm. Grab artisan sriracha or grass-fed jerky from their website.
www.farmtopeople.com

GENERAL GROCERY ITEMS

Thrive Market is an online marketplace for organic and non-GMO products that's easily searchable by dietary needs. You can pick up pantry items at reasonable prices as well as ecofriendly household goods and healthy snacks. Bonus: Become a member and you donate a membership to a low-income family, teacher, veteran, or student.

www.thrivemarket.com

SEAFOOD AND SEAWEED

We use the Monterey Bay Aquarium **Seafood Watch** app every time we buy seafood to check on the sustainability of a fish species. The website can also point you to more sustainable local businesses, from supermarkets to restaurants, that have committed to helping conserve ocean resources.

www.seafoodwatch.org

Maine Coast Sea Vegetables sells sustainably harvested seaweeds from the North Atlantic and is a good source for kombu, wakame, and other products mentioned in this book.

www.seaveg.com

MEAT

Your local farmers' market is a good place to start looking for a sustainable meat purveyor, but if you haven't yet found someone nearby, our friends Heather and Brad at **The Piggery** ship their pasture-raised pork, charcuterie, and deli meats around the country.

www.thepiggery.net

MISCELLANEOUS DELICIOUSNESS

Irene's old environmental science teacher Tina makes excellent maple syrup at **Bobo's Mountain Sugar** in Vermont.

www.bobosmountainsugar.com

INDEX

ABOUT THE AUTHORS

Margaret, Irene, and Andrew Li are the sibling co-owners of the The Mei Mei Group, a Boston-based restaurant, food truck, and catering company with a focus on innovation, sustainability, and great service. Led by Chef Irene, Mei Mei's creative Chinese-American cuisine draws on the siblings' multicultural heritage, combining Chinese techniques and influences with the bounty of New England farms. Their food truck, Mei Mei Street Kitchen, opened in 2012 and was soon awarded Boston's Best Meals on Wheels by *Boston Magazine*. Their brick-and-mortar restaurant opened in late 2013 and was named Eater Boston's Restaurant of the Year. Known for their dedication to sustainable operations, employee education, and ethical sourcing, including a commitment to serving only pasture-raised meat, Mei Mei has become a leader in the New England local food scene.

Margaret (aka Mei) currently lives in North Carolina, with her husband and daughter and an ever-growing collection of cookbooks and board games.

Irene is a four-time James Beard Rising Star Chef semifinalist, Zagat and Forbes 30 Under 30 Honoree, and Eater Young Gun. She loves rescue dogs and hip-hop dance videos, and lives in Boston with her husband.

Andrew enjoys grilling, binge-reading science fiction novels, and visiting every bouncy house in Greater Boston with his son, Jackson.